FEARLESS & DETERMINED

An Epic Solo Cycling Journey
from Nevada to Alaska

DAVID FREEZE

Published by:
Walnut Creek Farm Publishing
China Grove, N.C. 28023

Designed by Andy Mooney
Front cover photos by David Freeze and Jon C. Lakey
Back cover photo by Andy Mooney

ISBN 978-0-578-58503-1

FOREWORD

The word "grit" came to mind as I followed David Freeze's bicycle trip from Nevada to Alaska in the summer of 2019. Sometimes literal grit sparked the thought. David pushed on through choking dust, heavy smoke and gravel debris during different parts of the journey.

Most of the time, though, the grit of David's fearless fortitude was what left me shaking my head. Sure, he saw snowcapped mountains, lush fields and scenic waterways. But he also faced daunting obstacles as he pedaled up steep climbs, squeezed by tractor-trailers and camped outside in bear country — often while fighting off ravenous super-mosquitos.

Grit? Some people might call it stubbornness. Either way, once again David proved he has what it takes to reach a goal most of us would never attempt.

This trip to Alaska was not the first solo cycling adventure David has chronicled day by day for Salisbury Post readers. All told, he has covered more than 20,000 miles in 49 states on these journeys. It's hard to believe now how reluctant I was to share his enthusiasm in 2013, when he first proposed sending the Post reports from a cross-country trip. As editor of the paper, I'd heard lots of grand story ideas that ultimately fell through.

Obviously, I didn't know David very well.

I also didn't realize how many of the Post's readers take a personal interest in his daily reports. Sometimes he was writing about stomping grounds they still held close to their hearts; other times he told of places they longed to visit. Always, he shared down-to-earth reflections on the sights and people he encountered.

A wiry 66-year-old with single-minded purpose, David put his energy and resourcefulness to the test on this journey. He traversed 3,174 miles in 39 days.

Whether you followed his progress in the newspaper or not, you'll feel as though you're riding along as you read this book.

By far, this trip traversed the most remote areas David has traveled. Staying fed and hydrated was a constant challenge. He looked for sustenance wherever he could find it, and often junk food was the only thing available. Cycling all day burns about 6,000 calories, and sometimes much more, according to David. That's a lot of Reese's Cups and Pop-Tarts. A vegetarian for some 40 years, David added eggs, yogurt and fruit to his on-the-road intake whenever he could. When he's home on his horse farm near China Grove, though, he hardly eats sweets at all.

Trying to maintain communication from the wilds of

Canada and Alaska may have caused him the most frustration. Some of the companies he dealt with overpromised their services and left him hanging on hold again and again. A less determined person might have opted to let the stories wait so he could focus on the ride. But when David Freeze tells you he's going to do something, you can count on it. At the end of virtually every exhausting day, he wrote a report and sent it in.

For navigation, he relied on Milepost travel guide and the advice of people along the way. He also depended on a Higher Power that pulled him through tough situations more than once. "Lord, ride with me today" was his daily prayer. He also sought the help of prayer partners back home when conditions reached the lowest point. They faithfully lifted him up.

David Freeze has grit, all right, grit tempered with a spirit of gratitude. There's something humbling about not knowing where you're going to sleep the next night, or what you're going to eat. On every cross-country trip, David may be the only person on his bike. But one thing he knows for sure — he never rides alone.

ACKNOWLEDGMENTS

I say it over and over. Completing the book, with all the editing and setup, and supporting the ride are much harder than actually sitting on the bike seat and pedaling toward another adventure. Every day on the bike is exciting in some way, yet not every day writing and editing for hours could be considered exciting. In this section of the book, I get the opportunity to thank all those who played a part. Much more than that, I get to attempt an effort of gratitude to some of the finest people I know. It doesn't seem fair that I get to see the country and meet those along the way while this group must be content with just helping me do it.

The book team is solid again this year as Elizabeth Cook has taken over as chief editor and also provides the Foreword. Elizabeth was the editor at the Salisbury Post for many years, a post where she allowed me to explore my own interest in adventure and share the results with the paper's readers. Neither of us knew what path the first trip across the country would take and how much interest there would be. I think we have both had lots of fun along the way.

Andy Mooney is the rock star who pulls it all together. His knowledge and technical skills have made each subsequent adventure seem bigger and better than the last one once it hits the printed page. Andy always provides the stabilizing force when we hit snags, and his professionalism is amazing. Jon Lakey uses his photography skills time and again to enhance the finished product.

Providing logistical and technical support from home was Amanda Lewis. She found solutions and workarounds to allow the continuation of the shared adventure when we were at a loss to connect. Amanda took persistence to heart as she dropped her other activities to keep daily communication flowing back to Salisbury, especially from British Columbia, the Yukon and Alaska.

At home and on the farm, I got help from my family while pedaling away. My daughters, Ashley and Amber, and their husbands, Dale and Jamie, supported my travels, albeit with an occasional doubt or worry. My nephew and farm manager, Sammy Freeze, gets better each year at taking care of things with the animals and acreage. Mrs. Ollie McKnight helps out and makes sure all the details get done.

Rayna Gardner does amazing work as the scheduling and business manager of my adventures.

The Salisbury Post continues to allow me to document my travel while supporting my quest for all 50 states on a bike and more. There's a long list of friends and businesses that supported this trip. Mission Senior Living and Darryl Fisher from Carson City, Nevada, increased their involvement this year and provided the starting point. Others who helped make the trip happen were Father and Son Produce, Skinny Wheels Bike Shop, Men on Missions at First Baptist Church in China Grove, Accelerate Therapy and Performance, Gentle Dental, Vac and Dash, Gear for Races and individuals Dick and Jean Richards, David Post, Leonard Wood and Robert and Carole Hopkins.

Providing daily encouragement and prayers were the readers of the Post and an amazing number of friends from areas across the country and abroad. Connectivity problems in Canada and Alaska at times hampered the ongoing back-and-forth communication that I relish, but somehow we got it all done.

Proof that I never ride alone isn't hard to find. On this toughest journey yet came more examples of His power. I'm still overwhelmed at the rest area spring and the much-needed water in California, and how through prayer, my often unforeseen needs were answered yet again. Lord, continue to ride with me every day, on the bike, on foot and in any situation!

INTRODUCTION

I wanted to see a grizzly. Once into central British Columbia, I began to see black bears of all sizes. But I wanted to see a grizzly. Suddenly, coming off a long hill that had consumed most of my morning, I saw one walking quietly through a brushy area off to my left.

The grizzly was walking purposefully. Just before he stepped on the road, a tractor-trailer barreled by, missing the bear by only a half dozen feet or so. The bear spun around, gathered himself, and continued out onto the road just as I arrived. We looked at each other from 50 feet away, and I snapped his photo. At that moment, the bear changed direction and began to walk toward me. Only 30 feet away by then, I dropped the iPad into the bike's handlebar bag and started pedaling, figuring nothing good would come from waiting on the bear to arrive.

Not really concerned, I thought the bear would go about his business on across the road. I pedaled steadily for a few minutes until a small pickup with a dog barking inside pulled up beside me. The woman driver pointed behind us and said, "Look!" The bear was running after me, probably 20 feet behind.

Over the winter of 2018-19 back on the farm near China Grove and Salisbury, North Carolina, my restless spirit had peaked with the snows and winds during the season's short days. I needed something, and Alaska loomed ahead as part of my quest to reach all 50 states on a bicycle. Since Alaska was America's 49th state, I researched a route that would make it my 49th state as well. I didn't consider for a minute simply flying to the state; I wanted the whole adventure of riding from the lower 48 to Alaska, experiencing the people and places along the way. Having never visited British Columbia or the Yukon, I wanted to see them from the bicycle seat.

My previous long-distance cycling had been done in the U.S. and Canada, generally in areas that had supply sources and lodging for most days. "Be careful what you wish for" was a common theme when I mentioned my desire to ride to Alaska on a bike. Veteran travelers of the area warned of hills, mosquitos, horseflies and long stretches of up to 150 miles between supply points. How much harder could it be than crossing the Rockies, the Cascades or the Mojave Desert in the summertime?

Six years before, I wanted to discover America and find out more about myself along the way. I knew little about long-distance cycling. To be honest, I had fewer days in the previous 20 years on a bike seat than it would take to pedal over 4,000 miles across our country. I figured to just get on the bike and go, while learning along the way.

Totals of 48 states and nearly 17,000 miles had made for 218 days on the road, a different adventure associated with every one of those days. There is an incredible energy to waking in the morning and wondering what the new day will bring. Often totally worn out at the end of the previous day, I have never once awakened with the same feeling. And rest on some of those nights has been very limited.

I needed to push myself, to break out of the ordinary and fulfill an addiction to more adventure. And If I inspired others to go for their dreams, or just go outside and try new things, then all was well and good.

But for now, it's on to Alaska. More than 3,100 miles of unknown. Just the way I like it!

CHAPTER 1

Why?

May 2019 was a busy time back home. There was much to do, including a monster project on the farm that had to do with reworking an often-forgotten fence line. Most people wouldn't bother with what I wanted to do, recapturing the original fence area around a horse pasture that was likely to eventually cause trouble due to its poor condition. For many years, I had cows here on the farm and they were forever getting out, always at the worst times. Horses that learn to get out of a poor fence are even harder to handle, but they don't get out often, thankfully. I would be away for a couple of months and wanted things to go well.

Backing up a few months, I had decided to ride my bike to Alaska, setting out from Nevada. The background to this goes back eight years at least, beginning when I took a wild idea from a newspaper article and transformed it into a life-changing weekend in the Greenbrier River area of West Virginia.

Now all this time later, another major journey was almost upon me. Life for me is a series of challenges amid the quest for "Wow" moments. I had decided that I must finish this fence work before leaving on my next cycling journey. Each day, I found time out of an already busy schedule to work on the brush clearing, the wire and the posts. Probably what I wanted more than anything was to use the work time to sort through the upcoming bike ride and the crazy expectation of what likely would be a major trial. My bike touring experience was extensive now, but never had I been to large remote areas that rivaled upper British Columbia, the Yukon and parts of Alaska. Getting there through western Nevada, northern California, Oregon and Washington wouldn't be easy, but I had been to those states already. The unknown fueled my senses, always open to exploring new boundaries but preparing as best I could.

What began on that winter weekend on the saddle of a Trek mountain bike in West Virginia has become a controlled obsession of sorts. Before that, I had never considered riding a bike for any significant distance. The Greenbrier River Trail is spectacularly beautiful, remote and easy enough to ride. It is an old railroad line, now used as a rail trail about 80 miles in length. A dirt and crushed gravel surface fit the mountain bike fine, especially good since the Trek was the only functioning bike I had at the time. You see, I am a runner and consider running as my first identity. But the most important fact here is that I wanted something new and was ready to explore a new challenge. I was not sure just how big yet, but the door was open.

The three days spent on that trail and aboard the bike seat hooked me. Not experienced enough to know that late winter could be harsh on a bike, I pedaled through cold rain and a dusting of snow as I rode to the far end and back again. My gear fit in a couple of backpacks, one tied to the frame and the other on my back. The best story, shared often, is that I didn't know enough to balance properly while carrying that extra weight and immediately fell off the bike when mounting up to start the journey. A record time re-mount, just as if nothing had happened, got that show on the road and ultimately led to this new one too.

For the first few hours, I was amazed at nature's show, which appeared to be just for me. Over the three days, I saw only 12 other people on the trail. Signs warned of dangerous wildlife but none appeared. The green river water was so beautiful that I lost concentration a few times and drifted dangerously close to the riverbank drop-off. My goal of 55-60 miles a day seemed huge, as I had certainly never ridden that far. There was no real timetable. The day and the weekend were mine to experience.

What happened over those three exhausting days was the realization that I not only loved this but also wanted more. A lasting memory after loading the bike back on my truck at the trailhead seems as clear as yesterday. I was so tired, my shoulders ached, and I was hungry. But my mind was happy. And, as often happens when my mind is happy, I wanted more of what made it that way. Running has been that way for me too, as evidenced by the 86,000 miles already completed. But the question that surfaced in this case was how to get more of this adventure cycling thing.

Over the next few months, I didn't do much toward my new interest. I did some reading, and somewhere from that came the idea of this thing called the TransAmerica Bicycle Trail, all the way across this great nation. Dismissed at first as too much, especially for someone with just three days' experience, the thought didn't drift away.

Sharing the idea of a cross-country ride with the editor of the Salisbury Post, where I continue as a freelance writer, didn't go quite as I hoped. I wanted to ride and then report back to the paper for a continuing news story of sorts. She was lukewarm to the idea and appeared unsure that I would follow through. Arthroscopic knee surgery delayed a possible start for a year, but the time was right by 2013. I knew so little, but few mountains have remained too high to climb over the years. I could do this, couldn't I?

Fast forward, that cross-country ride did go well, and I learned about our amazing nation, and myself too. Oregon to South Carolina totaled over 4,000 miles of true adventure with the surprising result of embracing the people I met along the way. I am a true introvert, especially when unsure of what I'm doing, but the presence of the bike seemed to override my usual reluctance to talk. The amazing scenery was a bonus. The coverage in the local newspaper was a big hit, with my daily ride updates prompting communication with readers from the area and from around the country.

You can bet the hook had been taken and set with this first ride. Yet, all the resulting news was not good. A severe post-ride bout with blood clots caused major concern. Still, you could be sure I was going to ride again, even if against doctor's orders.

Next came a ride from Lubec, Maine, to Key West, Florida, going from the most eastern point in the United States to what is considered the southernmost city. A totaled bike from a car accident would have stopped this adventure had my family had their way. Blood clots again, probably this time caused by the collision, healed just fine. More medical visits proved that I didn't have the blood properties to cause extensive clotting. I would do it again.

On to the most fun of all the rides, America's Route 66 from California through the summertime Mojave Desert to Chicago. I continued on to Michigan and Indiana, with the idea of completing all 50 states on my mind. The tally of states was building, and I wanted more.

Next came the most historical ride, the Underground Railroad from Mobile, Alabama, to Toronto, Canada. Niagara Falls was all I expected and Canada too. By this point there was no question about going for more.

The area called the Northwest Tour in cycling terms, modified to include all the states from Washington to Wisconsin — with added ventures into South Dakota, Nebraska and Iowa — narrowed my needed states to just five. Nevada, Utah, Vermont, Alaska and Hawaii remained.

Nevada and Utah fell the next summer, including the "Loneliest Highway in America." Riding the Pony Express route and seeing a few of the great national parks made a wonderful two-week journey. Vermont fell, too, with a long drive to just bicycle in that state. I kicked myself multiple times for not taking a day or two to visit Vermont on the East Coast ride.

So the pieces connect, and we're back to that fence repair and Alaska on my mind. The weather was hot, and there was much to do before leaving the farm and Rowan County to head west for my Alaska ride to begin. As the days rushed by, almost every free moment was devoted to some aspect of the ride preparation or the fence repair, each as important in my mind as the other. I work part-time for Mission Senior Living in Carson City, Nevada, and my departure date was set for May 29. Just as I did last year, I would compete as part of a team for the Odyssey 178-mile event, running from Reno to Lake Tahoe and back again over what I hoped would be about 31 hours.

Spraying, chain saw work, stringing and rehanging fence wire, clearing limbs all amounted to a worthy physical workout in preparation for the upcoming adventure. My daily running was going well and I felt strong. Physically, I was ready. The details were getting done. As the remaining days dwindled, I began to focus on making sure that my bike was shipped to Carson City, and that a few remaining pieces of gear were replaced or added. Some of it was shipped ahead too.

New this year were a couple of solar chargers that would serve mainly to store extra battery power for my new Apple iPad Mini 5, an incredible device and the most important part of my planned communication back to the newspaper. My iPad Mini version 2 had served its purpose, and the new capabilities and enhanced camera of the version 5 excited me, especially if I could figure out how to use them as intended. Much of my ride would be in remote areas this time, without either electricity or cell coverage, and having the extra capacity mattered. The solar chargers could be attached to the back of the bike, probably riding on top of the tent and charging as I rode.

Besides the iPad and solar chargers, I didn't have many other new things. One purchased item that I hoped would not be needed was an over-the-head mosquito net. Large, aggressive mosquitos figured in stories read and rumors heard. I didn't buy any mosquito spray because I just don't like the stuff.

A new pair of cycling shorts had been ordered and received, my first with a loose fit and pockets. Contrary to popular belief, long distance riders don't change cycling shorts daily for a fresh pair, so be assured that this new pair would be worn every day. Washing by hand would likely be the only way to clean them on this trip.

A new cycling shirt and a better quality rain jacket, both in bright colors, were two more additions. Both seemed to satisfy what I needed, but only time would tell.

Returning for yet another adventure was my trusty Surly Long Haul Trucker bike, checked out by Skinny Wheels Bike Shop in Salisbury and deemed ready to ride. The Ortlieb panniers, or gear bags, are veterans of all my rides and perfect for what I do. I also added a new handlebar bag in matching red and black from Ortlieb, this one with a magnetic closing system.

Back, too, were my trusty tent and mini air pad, sleeping bag and tool kit, all dependable and proven over 48 states so far. I had a decent helmet but knew that on the trip I would probably wear a floppy hat and ball cap as much as the helmet. Traffic was not expected to be much of a factor, and lots of sun and heat could be significant while still in the U.S. and occasionally later on.

One new purchase that was more important for this trip than any other was a water filter that would allow drinking water from a natural source in an emergency. Supply points were going to be slim as I progressed north, and several days would have none.

I also packed both the minimum amount of warm and cold weather clothes, including my mittens. There would be cold mornings and warm days, and everything in between. A pair of roomy New Balance shoes from Ralph Baker's shoe store was the last significant piece of gear. These shoes had passed their window of bounce for my running but were so comfortable that I was excited about wearing them on the cycling adventure. Uncomfortable shoes can ruin a ride, and I was confident that these would be fine.

I included little else besides extras of long and short sleeve shirts, socks, cotton gloves and hygiene items. I also had extra bike tubes, CO_2 cartridges to inflate them, and a backup tire pump. I needed as much room as possible for water and food.

At the end of the book, I will address how the gear all worked out, what improvements were needed and other issues. The gear will all be listed by manufacturer with specifics.

With all this in place and the farm about squared away, I was ready to head west and get another grand adventure underway. As you might guess, I couldn't wait.

CHAPTER 2

The ride begins —
Carson City, Nevada, to Summer Lake, Oregon

How could anyone not be excited about the day that I was launching into? It was a picture-perfect morning on June 4 in Carson City, Nevada, my jumping-off point. My bike was at Mission Senior Living's corporate office and so was I. My time here began the previous Thursday. Plenty of activities had followed in the lead-up to this magical morning.

My flight from Charlotte to Phoenix on Wednesday had been delayed by weather, sending the plane out over the Gulf of Mexico to avoid a major weather front and adding 40 minutes of flying time. The pilot kept saying that he couldn't get air control to give him a quicker route. I didn't mind much, even after the flight arrived too late to make my connector to Reno. Near the back of the plane, I had no chance to get off the plane and change terminals in time, but I tried. So did six others who ended up at the same problem desk I did. Most of those ahead of me found ways to still get where they needed to be, although two agreed to share a car. My next available flight would leave very late and I was advised to take the early flight the next morning. A short shuttle ride ended at an affordable motel, and I enjoyed the relaxing evening.

With better results on Thursday morning, I flew to Reno and arrived by 9 a.m. My friend from Carson City, Darryl Fisher, was already at the Reno airport, flying veterans in one of his foundation's planes. Darryl is president of Ageless Aviation Dreams Foundation, an amazing story of how life's challenges result in unforeseen magic. (The story is chronicled in my book, Young Again, available at Amazon.) One of the Mission Senior Living locations had arranged flights for that morning. Once again, I got to be part of the experience. My memories of volunteering with AADF were wonderful and incredibly rewarding. An impending storm arrived just as the ceremony of the flights was drawing to a close. We left the airport and headed to my home for the next few days at Darryl's house.

My second Odyssey Run, a team challenge to complete 178 miles of running from Reno to Lake Tahoe and back, was the first big thing on the agenda. The run began on Friday morning, although my portion didn't kick off until early that afternoon. My legs of the journey, shared by 11 other team members, were certainly challenging and ended up totaling just over 14 miles. Mission Senior Living's team beat last year's total time by about an hour. With the finish line celebration completed, my focus shifted to final preparations for the ride to Alaska.

My bike had been shipped to The Bike Smith in Carson City, and all looked great when I picked it up. I had questions and small purchases in mind. I needed a few CO2 cartridges to top off my supply and was curious about a chain replacement link tool. Knowing that the ride would be hilly and very remote, I bought a replacement link, light and small in itself. My concern was whether I could actually reconnect the bike chain if it broke and needed the link replacement. I bought a used chain tool, a little heavier than I had hoped, from one of the bike techs. He told me how to use it. Should the bike chain come apart, I would be at least reasonably capable of repairing it. More likely to be an issue on this ride due to the lack of bike shops and towns in general, reconnecting the chain was one more thing checked off my list.

Top of the list was concern over my connectivity once the ride became remote. I knew from experience that AT&T and Verizon both had issues in less-populated areas. My cell phone carrier was AT&T and my iPad was on Verizon. My email server was Windstream. Some mix of these had to work for transmission of my daily updates and photos for the newspaper and answering personal emails along the way. All three of the companies had assured me that I would be in good shape. In Carson City, I stopped at the AT&T store for one more in-person conversation from a western U.S. perspective. The store tech left me to contact others for answers and came back to say, "You are good, for at least most of your intended travel."

I serve as the wellness coordinator for the staff at Mission Senior Living, and one of my responsibilities is a Tuesday morning conference call with the leadership group. My plan was to complete that call and then saddle up for the first day of the ride. As excited as I was, so were several members of the Mission leadership group who came out for photos as I was about to depart. Their support was wonderful, especially because none of my previous rides had included a send-off.

Darryl and I had checked the best route out of town toward Reno by car. His route was timely and got me on the old major highway, U.S. 395, in sight of the interstate but with little traffic. I stopped by a convenience store, I think the first one I saw, to get snacks for the ride. That first store wouldn't take a credit card; it turned out to the be the only one like this on the whole trip. I immediately wondered if credit card refusal would be a thing, but I had more cash than ever with me.

It took climbing a big hill to leave Carson City as the day warmed. None of that mattered because I was finally on the way to Alaska. Hanging over my head was the shorter riding day to reach Doyle, California, the only town of any sort within my range. Over the last few days, I had searched the internet for a motel, especially after a clerk at the Doyle convenience store said there was one. I found old references to a motel, only to call and find it didn't exist anymore. Other references pointed to a quality campground that actually posted lodging options.

Old U.S. 395 was very scenic, usually with shoulders, while it remained light on traffic. Rural scenery with snow-capped mountains and a river, with a mostly flat road, made for wonderful riding that morning. For about 25 miles to Reno, I was amazed at the stunningly beautiful surroundings. What a way to start!

I knew that Reno had lots of traffic, and sometimes there was nothing resembling a shoulder. I rode the length of Virginia Street, the main drag, and passed plenty of gambling casinos and high-rise hotels. All in all, passing through the busy city was easy enough, partly because bikes could use the bus lanes.

Exiting out the northern side of Reno was another story. The traffic picked up and so did the tougher terrain. More climbs and plenty of off and on ramps suddenly made cycling a bigger challenge. On busy ramps, I have always found it better to dismount and run the bike across when an opening develops. This can get tricky, especially with double ramps. A wide shoulder helped my riding in the busier traffic.

After I crossed into California, I felt the ride was finally underway. Making good time because of few hills, I was funneled into an inspection station. Two officers were stopping every car and talking with the drivers. A female officer just waved me on through with a smile.

My first real stop was a place called Hiawatha Junction, a sort of truck stop with food and gas for cars. I began to realize that supply points would quickly stretch out, and this midday stop would soon be considered a treat. The store was first-class and very busy, with plenty of items I wanted for my bag. Still, I expected that Doyle would have a food source too. No need to overload, as I would have to later. As a first in a long time, the happy clerk allowed me to fill my water bottles with free ice. Many stores along the major cycling routes allow this, but most of the others want you to buy a cup of ice. The ice was a big pickup for me as the day was really heating up, with hills growing and winds increasing.

Something happened with those weather conditions, though. Over the last 20 miles, the winds began to abate, and clouds covered the hot sun. Just as much of the early ride that day, I soon had 20 more miles completed in near-perfect conditions.

Doyle came into view, or at least part of it did. I couldn't really tell what was Doyle; some of it was off a side road and other things were still on U.S. 395. I found the highly touted campground and immediately went to the office. A light was on inside and I kept knocking on the door. Nobody came out and the door was locked, which seemed odd. There was some activity around and even a few campers. I realized that the majority of the campers looked permanently placed.

At that point, I heard Pamela Wells say no one was in the office. I walked over, and this friendly woman told me that she could call the owner if I wanted to stay. I asked about the lodging advertised on the sign. "Oh, there is nothing like that anymore," she said. Pamela called the owner and I learned I could camp for free if I didn't need power. The campground in general was in bad shape, with tall grass and gravel. Nothing looked too inviting, so I asked about sleeping on a picnic table. The owner didn't want us to move the only one in sight from one particular camper. Evidently there was a history involved with that table. I tested it and found it weighed too much to move anyway.

Setting up my tent here didn't seem inviting at all, although I would later sleep in much worse places. The solution came from Lynn Bobillot, another full-time resident. She had a pickup and offered to let me sleep in the back of it, plus she let me use some old couch cushions. I placed my sleeping bag on the cushions and looked for other ways to finish off the day. I could see the convenience store but had food in my bag. A veggie burger, made the day before, tasted wonderful. So did a few of the snacks I had picked up earlier.

Not really picky usually about a bathroom, I discovered the one available to me was definitely low-end. It was dark, had not been cleaned in months, and actually looked as if a good wind would take it down. Since nobody else was overnight camping, it appeared I was the only one who had used this bathroom in quite a while. There was no place to wash up, and the shower didn't look usable.

What I did find was a fairly nice laundry room, with available electricity. I sat on a bench in front of this area and typed my report for that night, eating more food and charging my iPad as I wrote. Things were looking up. My first tangle with a light dose of mosquitos was only a minor irritation. When finished, I headed for bed in the truck and slept away most of the night after some of the residents stopped driving around. Day 1 was in the books! I had made Doyle and completed 74 miles and felt great to be back on the road.

For most of the upcoming ride, I would be choosing my route based on available information. On this first segment, all I had was a series of state maps and a MapQuest suggestion of the best route. Getting to British Columbia seemed easy enough, and I planned to gather information near the Canadian border on how to proceed. But first, the rest of California, plus Oregon and Washington, were in my sights.

Day 2 got off to a climbing start on U.S. 395 again. There were some towns ahead, but my maps were oddly off on agreeing on the best route. It was my first day of a fierce headwind, something I didn't expect. By bypassing Susanville, I saved about 10 miles of riding by following a small road to Standish. Standish had a nice convenience store and I stocked up. Two locals, Sam Porter and Matt Long, told me of camping and lodging about 40 miles ahead, something that surprised me. They also warned of a steady climb. A worker at a rest area verified the campground idea, and I felt pretty good that I could find a good place to spend the night.

The ride out of Standish climbed about 1,000 feet to 5,000 feet before settling down. I have relied on prayer often when trouble lay ahead. My water consumption had been high on this warm and windy day, and I was dangerously close to running out. No supply points were near. Already rationing my consumption, I stopped to pray that there would be a water source soon. I had the water filter system but didn't yet see any moving water that looked worth using. It had been a long and challenging day, and the scenery was nothing like yesterday. I rode on and saw the signs for a closed rest area. While most western U.S. rest areas don't have potable water, I prayed that this one still would. Concrete barriers blocked cars from entering, but it was easy on a bicycle. Not really surprised, I found a still-working pipe supplied by a natural spring. I filled my bottles and drank to my content. Oatmeal cookies made for a great snack. The water tasted great. My prayers had again been answered.

Just a few miles ahead, I had topped out another hill and was stopped to plan my next move. I saw fire vehicles at a Bureau of Land Management station and noticed that another vehicle was turning in. The driver asked if I needed anything and told me to come get water if I needed it. Ryan

Rodd took me into the station and made me a huge peanut butter sandwich. Another firefighter gave me a big bag of almonds. Ryan heard my story and told me his. He had graduated the University of North Carolina at Greensboro, about an hour's drive from my home, and then he came west to be a firefighter.

Back on the road, I had no idea where I would spend the night. The towns of Ravenwood and Termo were ahead. There should also be a campground, based on earlier information. The wind had intensified again and I hoped to find something soon. A California Highway patrolman stopped to check on me, probably because I was riding with my head down against the wind. He was the first law enforcement person I had seen, and he took time to describe what to expect ahead. Both towns had nothing, he said, and the campground had no water and was way off the road. None of those options sounded good. "There is a gravel stockpile about 10 miles ahead," he said. "You would be safe to camp there if you want. Nobody will bother you." I immediately thought about sleeping in a truck the first night and on gravel the second, not exactly what I had planned.

Just after the patrolman left, I found the abandoned town of Termo and looked around. There was a building that I could sleep in, but it smelled bad and was filled with junk. I sat down and wrote my daily update while I had daylight and an unusually good Verizon connection for my iPad. When I was done, it was on to find the gravel area.

I had also passed a motel that had been closed and partially converted into housing. Later I thought it would have been worth my while to stop and see if they had a room or if I could camp there. I did not see a person but did see a truck.

Pushing pretty hard for those last few miles, I found the gravel stockpiles just before dark. It was dry and hot, and I decided to go ahead and camp there. Nobody was around. Only an occasional truck passed by. At this point, snakes had not become a worry. They would later.

After 87 miles on Day 2, I slept reasonably well on a giant pile of gravel. The town of Likely and a store were just 20 miles ahead. I was starting to get excited about the towns and stores that lay ahead, but a degree of uncertainty was developing. Available, dependable information was part of the issue, and of course connectivity. Siri couldn't help much if neither the cell phone nor iPad was connected.

I was surprised, too, at how cold the nights had become after hot days. My sleeping bag didn't seem to be up to snuff. I later realized that instead of swapping the bag for a thicker one that would be harder to carry, I should just put on more clothes. I was going to bed hot and waking up cold. The gravel morning was 46 degrees and windy, so not really that cold.

My first goal on Thursday morning, Day 3, was to find the store in Likely. I needed some things. I rode into the small town, immediately found the old hardware-looking store and was disappointed to find it closed. Other locals and travelers stopped by too, and I learned the store didn't open until 9 a.m. Realizing that the proprietor probably lived inside, I saw the lights come on and heard the door unlock. The owner was pleasant and had good prices on snacks and water, both of which were in short supply in my bags. After that stop, my energy kicked in and I pushed through another 20 miles on U.S. 395 toward Alturas.

Hills began to increase, and one took me back up to nearly 5,000 feet in elevation. Especially odd for California was that they did not name the summits, and the elevation signs were never placed at the top. Most states are proud of those summits. I have been too, after pedaling all the way to the top. Nothing feels better than to summit, catch your breath with a water and snack if needed, and then usually have some easier riding on the downside.

For such a dry area, there were several huge lakes. One of them was Goose Lake near Lakeview, Oregon. I was now in one of my favorite states from previous rides. Oregon is a very long state with everything from coastal areas to plains and mountainous areas. Great memories from my cross-country ride included scenery that would easily work in the best old westerns.

A side wind had developed, coming from the west — strong enough to push me to the side. I had to be careful in tight quarters and near low guardrails. Most guardrails are only knee-high on a bike, and the strongest wind could easily push a skinny cyclist over with the proper gust.

New today were regular sightings of rattlesnakes, most of them squashed flat by vehicles. Two were not dead. One of them surprised me during my snack and water break by crawling within six feet of me. Before I could get my iPad out for a photo, he was gone down a hole near the guardrails. The second was stretched out and ready to cross the road but sensed somehow that I was coming by and stopped just briefly. I rethought my easy decision to sleep on the gravel the night before, especially since they seemed drawn to the pavement. I couldn't remember ever seeing a live rattlesnake outside of captivity.

I was excited to near Lakeview with the likelihood that I could stay in a motel. The motels seemed numerous, but the first two I called didn't have a vacancy. Heavy clouds, suddenly cool temperatures, a heavy rain and early darkness all made for a much different ride into town. I was soon very cold and was a little late in stopping to put on my rain jacket. Riding into town among heavy traffic in low visibility was uncomfortable too. I coasted under a convenience store overhang and made a couple more calls to find yet another full motel and a recommendation for one that had rooms. With no answer there, I went ahead and rode on to the Interstate Motel while the chilly rain continued to fall.

The motel looked a little rundown. I didn't care; I was focused on getting out of the rain. Unclear as to where the front desk was, I found the restaurant door closed. Behind the next door I found a man behind a desk. A haggling session ensued, based on available rooms and where the WiFi worked best. I was freezing and needed to get it settled. He wanted $80. We settled on $60. My room was OK; everything worked. Best thing was a grocery store across the road and a good heater in the room. I was soon comfortable and settled in. My first shower since Tuesday morning helped things.

Lakeview is billed as the tallest town in Oregon, with an elevation of 4,800 feet. In 1900, a fire destroyed 64 of the 66 buildings in Lakeview. Somehow, the town survived.

I knew there was much to do when I got up the next morning. Crossing Oregon from south to north would be a challenge. I awoke to find a strong wind from the north that was predicted to blow all day. I left Lakeview and pedaled toward Valley View, 18 miles away. A store near Valley View was odd, to say the least. No vehicles were parked there, but I still wanted to stop for a break from the wind. A woman appeared from a dark wall in the corner as I perused the boxes of products, most of which were empty. A few small purchases were all I wanted, and I continued on.

U.S. 395 left me, and I began with Scenic Oregon Highway 31. The wind pounded and was worse when one of the many hay-hauling trailers came barreling toward me. The only interesting thing was plenty of beautiful hay fields as I rolled on toward Paisley. I continued to try to find a room with only the promise of a back room in Summer Lake, but

I was happy for that. "We'll find a room for you somewhere, even if it is a storage room or the conference area," the manager said. I appreciated that attitude.

My first flat of the trip, on the fourth day, happened a couple of miles outside Paisley. Several folks stopped to talk, with one motorcycle rider leaving me a can of Slime to fill the tube if needed. Slime is a gunky substance that supposedly fills holes. What was already a long and trying day had been made longer by the tire, and I was happy finally to be rolling toward Paisley. I envisioned a real town but found only a mercantile, or general store, a bar and a few small shops.

I bought a few things in the store and asked about a room. Two women tried to help me get an Airbnb room that was sometimes available. They found it already taken for this night. My only choice would be rolling 28 more miles into a howling wind that wouldn't let up. That ride took four long hours, during which I got a call that a room had opened up in Summer Lake. I wouldn't have to use the back room after all. A big break. This frozen Popsicle rode into the lodge area at 9 p.m.

Along the way, I had seen the Albert Rim, a 250-foot-high cliff that lasted for miles. I was sad to have missed Oregon's only geyser, the Perpetual Geyser. I never saw the sign, probably because I was pedaling head-down into the wind.

Once I knew I had the room, I worried that I couldn't get

there before the office closed. I was able to call at a point of good reception and paid by credit card. They would in fact be closing the office at 8 p.m., and I wouldn't make that. I was able to get the promise of two grilled cheese sandwiches and an order of fries waiting in my room. These were surely very kind people, and I hadn't even met them yet.

After a wonderful night and fantastic meal at the Lodge at Summer Lake, I was a little slow to get going the next morning. The room had baseboard heat, and I rigged up a chair to hold my shorts to dry. I had washed them out in the shower. Since they were just a little damp and it was 32 degrees outside, I gave them a few extra minutes.

The folks at the lodge told me the reason for the tight motel situation in the area. Birding was in full swing, and I saw evidence of it as I rolled the bike out the door. Lots of folks with binoculars and hiking shoes were walking the area, the most beautiful I had seen yet. I heard a chorus of birds chirping and wondered if there was something special about this area to attract them.

It was time to go, on this amazingly beautiful morning. The stay at the lodge had been almost magical. One thing that I found odd, but didn't bother me at all, was that the TV had only one channel, and it was controlled by someone in the lodge office. I had never seen that on any of my trips, but I would hear of it again later on this ride. Throughout this whole adventure, I cared little to watch TV on the rare occasions that I had a motel room.

As I walked the bike out of the room, I saw the woman next door as she closed her door and grabbed her binoculars. Since I had arrived so late the previous evening, I didn't see much of the immediate area. I was drawn to the promise of the meal that waited in my room. I had spotted my room from a distance, knew that the door was open, and didn't stop riding until the door was just a couple of steps away.

It would have been possible to blame my mistake of turning the wrong way on all these things, but I can't. I just walked out to the road and began pedaling in the direction that seemed right. I never do this, especially with only one road in play. Once again, having missed some of the scenery in the previous day's late evening light, I didn't really mind. Low clouds hung in place to block off the tops of nearby mountains, and the birds kept singing and chirping. Then I saw the Harris Schoolhouse. Built in 1890 and located just three miles from the lodge, it looked just like one that I had seen the previous night. At that point, I realized that I had ridden the wrong way. OK, I thought, if I had to do it, this was the perfect time. I actually had a gentle tailwind when I turned back to the north.

A little more about the schoolhouse: It served the area until a bus was purchased to take students to nearby Paisley. In 2002, a wildfire burned the surrounding area and miraculously did not damage the school.

Next came climbing over another unnamed mountain on that beautiful morning, just ahead of a long flat stretch with little traffic heading into Silver Lake. In 1894, Silver Lake had 43 people die at a Christmas Eve party, all burned to death in the same building.

Silver Lake had a nice convenience store and an operator to match. I loaded my bags for the ride to La Pine, where I planned to spend the night. Continuing on the Oregon Scenic Byway, Route 31, the next 48 miles earned the name proudly. I began to ride the most beautiful road yet, with a large snowcapped mountain straight ahead. My first wildlife sighting was two magnificent elk that ran across the road ahead of me and disappeared over the next hill. Still miles away from the mountain, Oregon 31 came to an end and I took a right on U.S. 97.

I saw signs for Fort Rock, a volcano bed relic that resembles a fort. In an area popular for fossil hunting, there are several dormant volcanoes. Nomads were thought to have inhabited the area at least 11,000 years ago.

La Pine was the first town, and I spent the night there at the Valley View Motel, one of the first without air conditioning. Very similar to an old Route 66 Motel, it had a bigger-than-usual bed area and a very small bathroom. A good sign was the bottle cap opener in the bathroom. This was a wonderful day for my riding, including favorable temperatures, good terrain and nice road shoulders. I could have easily stretched on to more than 100 miles for the day. Afraid to miss a good motel, though, I had called and booked the last room about midday. One contributing factor was that my bike was not shifting correctly on two gears and I wanted to try to figure it out. A bike shop was just ahead in Bend, Oregon, if I couldn't. Had I extended the riding, I would have hoped to use those faster missing gears.

I asked about food in La Pine and was told there as a grocery store across the road and several restaurants nearby. None of the restaurants appealed to me, and the grocery was a wholesale one, offering large sizes of most everything and not a lot of choices. So I set out walking and looked for more. I found an open restaurant but not a person in it, or at least nobody came out. I walked back out, checked out a couple of slack convenience stores and settled on a pretzel and ice cream place. Those items, plus things I had in my bag, were my dinner for the evening. Some would have been disappointed, but I was not. As I rode past this area the next morning, I realized that just a half a block farther was a huge regular grocery store. I didn't stop that morning either.

The morning was 28 degrees, and I had turned the heat on just briefly in the room. The flags were gently blowing toward the north, signifying a tailwind. The bright sun made the air seem warmer than it was. After a brief stop at McDonald's, I shed my long pants and mittens.

I pedaled toward Bend, about 30 miles away, with a series of snowcapped peaks to my left. The only challenging climb was over La Butte Pass, at something over 4,000 feet. As soon as I could, I called ahead to Hutch's Bikes and found they were open on Sunday. I pedaled on to find it and to see one of the fittest cities on the planet.

The morning was bright and beautiful and actually warmed more. For the first time on my trip, I got directions on my phone to the bike shop and had Siri talk me to the front door. Hutch's Bikes was in one of those trendy areas with lots of little coffee shops, restaurants, runners and cyclists. I stopped in to see Holly Wenzel, whom I recognized as the voice on the phone, and told her I was the person who just called. The shop was hopping. My bike was slotted a little down the list of those to repair, but Max Lowenstein assured me he would get to it quickly. "Just tell me what is wrong, go get some breakfast, and I will call you when it's ready," he said.

I grabbed my wallet, phone and iPad and left the rest with Max. Bend is a city of 90,000 residents, where bike lanes take precedence over street parking. Few things bother me more than to find a car completely blocking a bike lane on a busy street, forcing a cautious ride into traffic to get around it.

Beside the big shop was a fantastic bagel shop. I am a huge fan of big and reasonably priced bagels, especially those still warm when I get them. Bag-o-Bagels was my kind of place. I bought enough bagels to eat on the spot and have a few left over for the ride. They had great brownies, too, and I got a big one.

I sat on a picnic table and ate while arranging a room for

the night. Watching people was fun too, but they all seemed to be in their 20s. Is that a requirement of trendy?

Max called and said the bike was ready. The short walk of about a block didn't take long, and immediately Max told me he had fixed the problem with a spacing adjustment. He also put a tube in the rear tire. I bought three more tubes for the road. The service was wonderful, very timely, and I was on my way riding north within an hour of first stopping.

I was now continuing on U.S. 97 and would remain with it much longer than I originally planned. One big hill and a few short ones, along with plenty of flat riding, took me into Redmond, another significant town of about 25,000. I kept riding to the north into beautiful and often irrigated farmland. A wonderful 76-mile ride brought me to Madras, a town of 6,000 that seemed much bigger, with a lot of chain stores in sight. I tried to grow alfalfa on my own farm years ago and marveled at all the beautiful alfalfa hay drying in the field. There was even a field of large carrot plants being grown for seed.

It was hot that day in Madras. Actually, the locals thought it was hot, but I felt very comfortable. I found a great little motel and was suddenly craving breakfast for dinner. I saw the Brown Bear Diner nearby, with two bears sitting in an old pickup outside, and called to see if they still had breakfast. They did, and I got the works. The bag weighed about five pounds. The veggie omelet and a pancake cost a surprising $18, but for once I didn't care. I was off the road at a reasonable time after another good riding day and had plenty to eat. What more could I want?

Ice was one thing I still wanted, and again I heard that this motel didn't have ice. I was passing out of the area where ice would be available.

In the daylight, I saw a woman sleeping on the gravel outside of a bar. She hardly moved, and several people were watching her. I took a picture and moved on, wondering if she liked sleeping on the gravel more than I did. I came upon a beautiful, deep river gorge and stopped to make photos. I bet the people in cars wondered what I saw to take photos of. Madras was a cool little town, but it was time to go. A week of riding was complete and my third state was coming to an end later today.

U.S. 97 merged with U.S. 26 just past my motel, and big trucks had run by all night, something that was oddly comforting to me. But early in the morning, I was glad to see most of them taking 26 as I continued on 97. Oregon was coming to an end, and Washington was just ahead.

CHAPTER 3

Madras, Oregon, to Oroville, Washington

Two nights of sound sleep had energized my legs. My body felt good too, and I expected no supply problems for a few days. It was easy to be excited about the next segment of the trip. Not far ahead, the terrain would be even more remote. For now, I had to finish Oregon and I was focused on Biggs Junction for the evening.

Madras had been good for me. A few hours off the road, plenty of good food and sleep — always in short supply — were rejuvenating. I'm not known as someone who needs much sleep in my normal day-to-day life. On these cycling adventures, I need way more than I am willing to take time to get. The excitement of what lies ahead always has pulled me out of bed. I hope it always will. This works at home too.

Just before leaving Madras, right after the traffic divided on 26 and 97, I wanted to load my bags. I noticed a big convenience store on 26 and its road out of town. I was only about two blocks away on 97, so I took a quick cut-through and went back to the store. The prices and selection were good, and I got plenty of stuff. At this point, I was still getting cookies, crackers and anything full of carbohydrates, the same things you can get around home in North Carolina. This would change soon too.

After loading my bags with water and food, I headed north with a secondary goal in mind. If I made good time — and that was a big "if" — the perfect ending to the day would be watching the NBA Finals. I am a big basketball fan and have long had season tickets at Davidson College. Stephen Curry provided some of the biggest thrills I have ever experienced in a basketball arena. After meeting him several times, I have stayed up way too late to watch the Warriors' games on the West Coast quite often. Now that I was on the West Coast, this game would start at 6 p.m. and I had a chance. Wind, hills and a little luck would all play a part.

Immediately out of Madras, I started a long and steady climb. As I passed through Willowdale, nothing much of note was happening except another beautiful morning. This one reminded me of a Rocky Mountain-type climb, long enough and steep enough that I could do it but was ready for the hard push to end as soon as possible. A huge paving project broke the tedium, and finally I cleared that too. Certainly, the view seemed to define the top of a formidable ridge.

Shaniko was more of a surprise than I expected. Signs told of a Wild West town billed as "Where the West Still

Lives." And it could have too. Founded in 1901, with a huge hotel and plenty of other old buildings, the town had a main street that looked as if two pistol-clad gunfighters might emerge at any moment. I read that some of the buildings were original and some were brought in from nearby areas. There was little traffic, so I took time to ride through town, which amounted to about three streets. I stopped at the general store and immediately wished I hadn't walked in. As the only person in the store, I noticed that the clerk watched every move I made. Nothing she had was high on my list, but I did buy a small Cosmic Brownie and a cinnamon bun. I hope my potential Little Debbie sponsors will read this. I was pretty sure that the store bought boxes of these items someplace else and then opened them up to sell one at a time.

Back on the bike, I thought about how wonderful it would be to get inside these old buildings with someone who could give a knowledgeable tour. I saw that Shaniko was once considered the "Wool Capital of the World." A woman sitting outside the antique store hollered at me and went back to her paper. Since I didn't understand her, I just kept riding.

The next town was Kent. Bright and sunny at midday, the town had not a soul moving around and no stores that I could see. What surprised me was that the area looked like a smaller and hillier version of Kansas. Grain fields and grain elevators, the places where they store the grain, dominated the landscape. After climbing again on a day that was never flat, I began a 12-mile gradual downhill into the wind and toward Biggs Junction on the scenic Columbia River.

Biggs Junction looks like a huge "fuel, eat, sleep as you pass through" type of place. There are half a dozen motels, several truck stops, multiple restaurants and convenience stores. I don't remember anything else. Not wanting to get shut out of a motel on such an important basketball night, I had called ahead to Dinty's Motel and reserved a room. The price was right, the room was wonderful, and it had a great view of the river. All these places to get food made me drool a little bit too.

I went right to the check-in desk and talked to Joe Griese and Nikkie Spaniola, who had earlier given me some travel insight for the day. They knew about the bike ride and the long 94 miles I had traveled that day. Nikkie thought I would get 100 from Madras, but I didn't. No matter, I checked in, got their photo and headed for the room. With just a half hour before game time, I wanted to grab a large volume of food and put my feet up while writing and watching the game — and the river too.

After rolling the bike into the room, I came back out and noticed that the folks in the next room were sitting across the parking lot from each other. I started to walk toward the food options when Denise Taylor asked me about the bike ride. I described it to her, and we were soon joined by her husband, Ben. Ben had been sitting in the sun near the motel door while Denise was in the shade across the lot. They were still carrying on a conversation, but as I left them, they both headed for the room. Especially interesting about the Taylors was that they were from La Claire, Iowa, home of the American Pickers and Mike, Frank and Danielle. Nice folks who I enjoyed meeting. There was just enough time to run over to McDonald's and get one of my favorite non-rushed dinners.

I love Egg McMuffins and learned long ago not to order them without the meat. It takes too long and some stores get all confused with that. I toss the meat or give it away, and I'm usually set. This time, I also got cookies, fries, a couple of pastries and ice cream, all the staples needed for long-distance bike riding. I immediately planned to get more ice cream after the game. Headed to my room, I noticed that the Taylors were back in their room with the door open because they saw me coming and restarted the conversation. I got their address so I could send them a book.

With so many tractor-trailers coming and going and a few more settled for the night, I noticed that most of them had big moose and bear bumpers added to protect the grill and some of the sheet metal. The trend as I continued north would be more of these. One small business the next day had 11 trucks of various sizes, with nine of them sporting the heavier and bigger bumpers.

Tomorrow was supposed to be in the 90s, and I had asked for extra water at McDonald's. Soon all that was gone. After the game, I headed out for more water and the extra ice cream. I felt great but dreaded the big climb up the hill on the other side of the river. Nikkie said, "At least 12 miles, maybe more!" I got the downhill today, so I would pay for it tomorrow. That climb would take most of the morning. I noticed the wind generators on both sides of the river were still going, even at 9 p.m. Regardless, Canada was getting closer.

While looking at the river, watching the game, eating, writing my update and relaxing, I had time to watch the lights of the tractor-trailers climbing the big hill on the other side. The lights looked cool, but I dreaded the climb even more. Up early that next morning, I was ready to get it done. But first, the motel had given me a coupon for one of several things at the store next door. I went in and ordered two egg and cheese biscuits, looked for a drink I liked and couldn't find one. I kept the coupon for a souvenir. The biscuits looked great and I went outside and had one right away. I was ready for the hill and topped the worst of it by 10 a.m.

There was a nice convenience store soon after, and I made two discoveries while there. Or I should say that I discovered Long Johns, the pastry. They had homemade ones right next to the cash register. I got one, then two. I ate one outside while Jackie Mahar came over to ask where I was going. I told her I was from North Carolina, had started in Nevada and was on a tight schedule to make Anchorage by July 12. Jackie and Dan were really interested and had some history or ties to all those areas. What really surprised me was their hometown of Adelaide, Australia, and the fact that they lived in a suburb called East Salisbury. I enjoyed yet another conversation, something that adds so much value to these trips. Most of the people I talk with probably think I am a tad crazy for doing these adventures, but that and the bike do seem to draw people. Once again, I was so wrong when I first said that the long bike rides would be about the scenery. The Mahars promised to follow the story online in the Post.

The clerk and a customer in the store both told me about yet another climb just ahead, promising it would be tough. "You will have to get over the Satus Pass first!" That was tough enough, but what really got me was a series of false summits. I was sure I had climbed to the top of the pass, but after a small downhill the road turned back up again. Finally, after a very long morning and into the early afternoon, I climbed over the top and settled in as U.S. 97 mostly flattened out for about 40 miles.

Up and over a steep butte, I began a descent into Toppenish, Washington. The hunt began again for supplies. Having made better progress than I expected, I thought a motel or two looked inviting. With that needed 80-mile average hanging over my head, I called ahead to Union Gap to see about a room in the Quality Inn. I saw online that I should be able to get a good price and did a little negotiating with Calista Morrison to do just that. I had been riding long enough to know that the art of getting a room was something that I had great enjoyment in doing. Seldom do I just say, "Fine, I'll take it!" Sometimes I struggle with tired legs to make the last town of the day, but I also know that $10 saved on a room goes a long way toward food or the next night's room. Sometimes I wonder if the desk clerk or even the owner might enjoy the exchange too. My standard line is, "I have 40 nights of this, can you give me a better price?" More times than not, I do get a better price or the tax included. That is another standard of mine. If the price seems a little too high, I say, "Is that with tax included?" They hesitate a little and then agree. No, it doesn't always work, but the percentage is good. And the tent riding on the back of my bike is a big bullet in my gun, especially for what this trip would become later. Plenty of camping was just around the corner.

Pushing hard on toward Union Gap, south of Yakima, I was especially excited to get a flat road and a gentle tailwind. That is the best kind of riding, leaving plenty of time and energy to look around. Still on U.S. 97, I had a slight dilemma coming up. My 78 miles today would leave me at the point of jumping on the interstate highway tomorrow for the first time on this trip. Nothing to worry about tonight, but the exit to the join the interstate was just outside my motel door. U.S. 97 joined the interstate to push through Yakima and on to Wenatchee. I had reached a major agricultural area, smack in the middle of cherry and asparagus production. About two more days, part of it riding upstream on the Columbia River, would have me at the entrance into Canada. I was ready.

One special moment on the ride today was the long-distance view of Mt. Hood at 11,245 feet, Mt. St. Helens at 8,365 feet, Mt. Adams at 12,307 and Mt. Rainier at 14,405 feet. Snow still covered them all.

I found the Quality Inn to be OK, not the best, but nice enough for the price and location. I also found breakfast next door at a Denny's. Denny's and IHOP stores are big. I crave the protein of the eggs and the carbohydrate energy of the pancakes. Loading for a big ride the next day works well this way. An hour after eating a giant breakfast for dinner, I would likely be hungry again anyway.

A close convenience store provided fuel for the early morning dash on the interstate. I rode the entrance ramp on up to the big road, along the way noticing a sign that said pedestrians were not allowed. Most states consider cyclists to be pedestrians. But I had done my homework, researching the State of Washington bicycle laws. Interstates 82 and 90, both just ahead on this bright morning, were not listed as off limits. I would explain that if stopped. But I also found the terrain initially suitable for faster riding times, so I pushed it. Crossing the rush hour ramps was the only thing that slowed my quicker pace on this morning. In a flash, 10 miles passed with only a couple of tight spots where old bridges didn't leave space for road shoulders. I pulled my own shoulders in and pedaled faster, and all went well.

I-82 gave way to I-10. I counted this day as the second most challenging so far, just behind the one into Summer Lake. Lots of climbing and very little scenery made for a boring morning, but the miles toward my entry into Canada were clicking away. A huge panorama of beautiful farm country changed that as I descended into Ellenwood. I had never seen major cherry production until this day. The trees were everywhere, heavily laden with bright red fruit. Tremendous stacks of forklift-sized boxes were evident along the sides of the road. Beautiful hay was being harvested too. I enjoyed this brief respite from climbing, knowing it was coming back again quickly.

My one meaningful conversation of the day was at a nice enough Conoco convenience store. The guy who seemed to be running the place waited on me, and I asked what was ahead. He replied, "Fifty-four miles of climbing, and Blewett Pass at the top of it is long and hard." When I asked about stores along the way, I got one of those replies that I laughed about later. "Well, I have always driven it in a car, so from a cyclist's point of view, I don't know," he said. What kind of answer was that? He made it worse by adding after some thought, "Yes, there are several stores along that route." There was not a single one for 58 miles! My water supply was dangerously low, but I knew that my home for the evening was Cashmere. A wonderful room in the Village Inn Motel was not far ahead. Pictures online made it quite inviting.

I was thrilled that the last 28 miles for the day were flat and downhill, and a gentle tailwind pushed me to a 14 mph average to knock out the distance in two hours. That is fast on a loaded bike and not common at all, so I arrived in town feeling pretty good, with a 100-mile day. About 800 miles of the nearly 3,200-mile journey were in the books. The day didn't get into the 90s as predicted. But another forecast for warm temperatures tomorrow might happen, since my elevation dropped about 3,000 feet during the afternoon.

With such a late finish on the ride this Wednesday, I stayed up eating things I got from a neighborhood grocery while writing my daily update. A rather comical situation developed in the store as I asked about the location of several staples, like potato chips in small bags. I almost never eat chips and a lot of my other favorite foods from the rides when at home. On this day and fairly often while riding, I felt the need for high fat. From my own nutritional training, I knew that fat often controls hunger urges. Maybe deep inside, I was looking for that. I bought enough food to fill one of my panniers. While buying it, the clerk asked where I was riding. The four or five other people in line all listened and encouraged me to keep it going, making a wonderful memory.

Another pleasant memory from Cashmere and the Village Inn Motel was the fact that the owner had to help me find it. For some reason, Siri had the location wrong, and it didn't clear up until I got closer. I had to call the motel twice to make sure I was on track. The Village Inn is a true family-owned motel, run by a bunch of wonderful Asian folks who genuinely care for the customers and keep the motel in first-class shape. They gave me the quietest room at the end of the building without my requesting it, just aware that I would need good sleep. And they had a working ice machine.

Back in the room, I stayed up until 11 p.m. finishing everything. I was pumped at the good output for the day and the overall solid start for the long journey to Alaska. Things were going well, and I took a little extra time that night to let God know I realized it.

Rewarding myself with 15 minutes of extra sleep and another quick stop at the store, I was about 30 minutes late as I headed north again on U.S. 97. My first target was Wenatchee and then East Wenatchee. Faced with a dilemma, I am still not sure if I made the right choice. Alternate 97 took the west side of the Columbia River, while most of the traffic and all the big trucks seemed to choose the regular U.S. 97. Most of the fruit trees were on the U.S. 97 side, and I just followed my MapQuest directions to continue that way. For miles, I could see the few cars on the Alternate side riding a flat road down next to the water. Buildings and fruit trees blocked most of my views, and the road was up and down. The route was not severely challenging, but higher traffic, lesser views and what climbing there was didn't reinforce my choice. My map showed no bridges for miles to cross the river. I was committed to make the best of it.

Eventually I lost sight of the Alternate 97 road and thought maybe it had ended. Later I realized it was still there but had climbed to the top of a significant ridge on the other side, much more challenging than my side. Amazingly, my side became easier to ride, and the views of the river improved as at least some luster of the main 97 returned.

The community of Orondo, Washington, came next, and I eventually crossed the river on a major bridge at Chelan Falls. At the same time, I could see the road on the other side quite a distance above us and was dreading the climb up there. I could see considerable traffic on it. The temperature was climbing too, and the breeze was almost non-existent. Passing the Wells Dam as part of a 40-mile stretch without supplies, I was quickly running out of water. I noticed a little park overlooking the dam. I thought about doubling back to check for a water point but didn't, with some re-gret later. The temperature had reached 96 degrees as I drew close to Pateros, already planned as the end of my ride for the day. With a great view of the town, I stopped to sip my last water about 3 to 4 miles from the town. I saw a rest area too, but clearly it didn't have any water either. I was toast, but the town was close.

As it turned out, one of the first buildings in town was a convenience store — big, modern and well stocked. I had traveled only 64 miles, way less than the day before, but was close to done for. I could have refueled and done more later, but the tank was empty at arrival time.

I already had a second floor room overlooking the river and it wasn't far away. Pateros was not large but still was much bigger than most of the towns I had come across. None of this mattered as I parked the bike and stumbled into the store and the beginning of another experience. Two clerks were helping the steady stream of customers, and a smiling girl offered to help me. I already had a couple big waters, some ice and some food, but my focus was on the ice cream. It seemed to be sold separately. I asked the girl what flavors she had, to which she replied, "We have lots, but the best deal is the soft serve machine. You can get all you want to fill the cup, depending on the cup you buy." I paid for my other stuff at high prices — not surprising since this was the only store in town — and also paid for the large soft serve cup. With my bag of other items in hand, I headed for the ice cream machine and loaded it with a chocolate and vanilla swirl. I started to walk out and the other clerk, a gruff guy with a headdress of some kind on, said, "Aren't you going to pay?" I said, "I already have; I paid her." The girl nodded in agreement. I went outside in the shade, ate all that ice cream and drank a bottle of water.

My energy returned and I headed on down to the motel, eager to get checked in and relax some more while off the bike. I found the Lake Pateros Motor Inn, where some type of shift change and new employee orientation was going on. Another customer was checking in, and everything was being used as training for the new employee. I waited patiently, not always easy to do but easier because of the ice cream upload.

Finally, I got the key to the room and took my bike and bags upstairs to see the beautiful view of the Columbia River. The Columbia begins in British Columbia and is the largest river by volume that enters the Pacific Ocean. It also is one of the oldest rivers in the world. I first met the Columbia when I arrived in Astoria, Oregon, to begin my cross-country ride in 2013. Astoria is near where the Columbia empties into the Pacific.

Pateros was the first stop for miles, and I was glad of it. Most of the town was destroyed by fire in 2014, and a major rebuilding project continues. I suspect that the convenience store and an attached restaurant were a part of that rebuilding. Both looked new. Over the years, there has been considerable flood damage here as well.

I was still trying to justify why things I needed cost so much. Regardless, a short time later I called the restaurant to check on the availability of a veggie burger. "Yes, I have one!" said a waitress. I asked how much and was told $18. I asked why so much, and she immediately offered a discount. I told her I would decide and let her know later.

The second part of the ice cream saga soon played out. Late in the day, the store was less busy, and the original clerks were not around. I bought more water, a couple of snack things and told the new clerk that I wanted to get ice cream. This time she sold it to me by weight. I got a free cup, filled it and brought it back to be weighed before paying for everything. A much smaller cup, less ice cream and a still-high price made up the package this time. She told me to sit down and enjoy it in the store, but I declined so I could go get the veggie burger next door. Eating the ice cream on the way back to the room, I vowed to wait until the next town to buy more supplies. Pateros had enough of my money already.

My dilemma when I got back was whether to sit outside and watch the river or go inside and get ready to watch the next game of the NBA finals — or some mixture of the above — while starting on my daily update. I sat outside for a while, then came back in and turned on the loudest air conditioning unit I experienced on the trip. This thing was so loud, I had to blast the TV, which led to the next problem. I turned on the pregame and the station had signal problems. The picture kept freezing up. I called downstairs and one of the girls came up to look at it, with no resolution. About then, the picture unfroze after turning the TV off and on again. This was the solution multiple times throughout the game that ended the Warriors' repeat championship chances.

With everything in place to leave Pateros the next morning and head to Oroville, my thoughts turned to crossing the Canadian border. I had called a bank in Oroville that agreed to exchange American cash for Canadian. It was down the street from the motel I took time to reserve too. I had to call and arrange the Verizon Travel Pass for international use before crossing into Canada. AT&T and Windstream had both assured me I would be good in most areas. Soon would begin issues that shot down all these assurances.

After the game, I went out to watch the lights reflect on the big river. I said a few extra prayers too, as I had one more day in the United States. Afterwards, I would be in Canada, both British Columbia and the Yukon, for about 1,600 miles, nearly twice the miles as I had covered so far. I wondered if I had done everything to this point to make the time in Canada work well. It seemed so, but we would know more soon.

On one of the warmest mornings of the trip so far, I left Pateros in short sleeves, pedaling into a very slight headwind. The sky was bright and so was the outlook for the next big stage of the adventure. The first six miles went quickly, and I spotted a McDonald's in Brewster. The fruit companies were very busy this morning, but few customers were in the McDonald's, an unusual thing. One guy got a cup of coffee while I asked about McMuffin prices and specials. Nothing was of major interest, so I got one McMuffin and a pack of cookies in the attached convenience store.

As I pedaled away, I noticed plenty of traffic into another store offering burritos and biscuits. More large fruit packing facilities were spaced along the road, with forklifts using the street to transport boxes of cherries. I noticed a small fleet of older, bulky helicopters, with all but one parked on the top of a hill. That one kept going back and forth out over some of the cherry orchards. I wondered why and later found out that the helicopters were used to dry the cherries. Cherries are susceptible to damage when it rains, sometimes causing the skin to split when rainwater is absorbed. Helicopters cost $1,200-1,800 an hour to operate, but cherries bring in $10,000 an acre, so it's big business to keep the cherries dry.

The Columbia River made a turn away from U.S. 97 and I picked up the Okanogan River, an agriculture water source, for the rest of this day's trip at least. My favorite riding days have often come when following a river downstream, especially one that meanders along. Best-case scenario happens when the river and the road comingle for a long distance; usually a steady downhill is the result. For my riding on this Friday, there was not a single significant hill all day. I wouldn't get many of these.

The next towns were Okanogan and Omak. I recognized the next section of travel from having crossed this area on my cycling tour of the Northwest in 2017. Wonderful memories flooded my mind, and I will share some of those. The Loup Loup Pass from Twisp was one the best and most interesting stories to tell. I heard major roadwork was going on in the area and that my route would be altered, adding at least 50 miles to get around it. Of course, 50 miles is a major change and in this hilly area would add most of a day. I didn't want that and planned to stop by the police station in Twisp and see what the real scoop was. I have a history of working through — or ignoring — road construction issues. It is easier to seek alternatives on a bike than to follow a long detour. The Loup Loup road had been severely damaged by a storm.

My stop at the police station went really well, as the chief arrived just shortly after I did. An upbeat and humorous guy, he suggested that I could get through the construction. He told me a passable road was open and gave me a card to document our discussion. After the needed food stop before a planned long climb, I easily found the detour sign. And several more. I met two locals who said the road had been closed for a long time and there was no chance to get through. One of them was quite snippy when I explained my desire to continue on and see what could happen. "I will see you coming back this way later," she said. "Nobody gets through!"

To shorten the rest of the story, I met some good folks who understood my dilemma, appreciated what I was doing and worked with me to get through in a very reasonable way. They left me with a significant physical challenge to complete, but if I could, then they agreed to support me as

I summited the pass and continued on over the other side. Fortunately, I never again saw the woman who was so sure she would see me coming back down.

I promised never to reveal the exact details and I won't, but I also was quite satisfied with the experience and the good folks I met.

Back to the current journey, I rode past the town of Riverside and into Tonasket, the actual intersection of the two routes. I spent the night on that first trip at the Red Apple Inn and loaded up on a day's food at the Junction, last seen at 6 a.m. on a morning when I had two major climbs up and over the Wauconda Summit and the Sherman Pass.

This time through, I stopped at the Junction again. It was just as busy as before. Alyce, who worked there on that first day, but not at the actual hour I stopped, was excited about my trip and promised to follow it. I got another Long John, quickly becoming hooked on them.

Excited too about the next stop, I found the door of the Red Apple Inn locked. A sign on the door said the owner was on the property and to call his number. Chris Zafares is 80 and a former marathoner, and one of the best discussions ever on my cycling adventures. We caught up on President Trump, my trip, his family and a lot more. Chris still walks three miles a day, and I know he enjoys the beautiful little town of Tonasket.

I kept seeing historical signs about the rich Indian history of the area and the important pioneer accomplishments.

It was certainly a beautiful area, especially for the second time through and my satisfaction at visiting with my own past, as well as talking to Chris and Alyce.

With my final destination in the U.S. looming ahead, I pedaled toward Oroville. I had booked a room at the Camaray Motel. Never sure of what to expect but always hoping to find good things ahead, I pedaled toward the small town. I hit the jackpot with wonderful owners Clyde and Sandy Andrews. Both were incredibly helpful in assessing my future route and possible issues, and Clyde eventually suggested a change in the route I had planned. He thought staying on 97, which would become B.C. 97, was safest and would have more service points. The room itself was everything I could expect, with a fair price and an amazing grocery store just a short bike ride away. I took advantage of all these things and gathered myself for the entry into Canada after today's 80-mile ride.

Most of my ride on this Friday was on the Okanogan Trail, and I saw that it continued into Canada. Once I crossed the border, I hoped to get some relevant information at the visitor center. I had my passport in my handlebar bag ready to use and nothing in any bags that should cause an issue with customs. I was just four miles away. I planned to call Verizon and start the Travel Pass on Saturday morning before leaving the motel. Nothing else was particularly on my mind, but I sure was excited about entering Canada and starting the most rigorous part of this adventure.

I knew that British Columbia and the Yukon would have challenges and experiences that I had never faced before.

I had no idea where I would end up on Saturday. Nothing about that concerned me. Let's go see western Canada!

CHAPTER 4

Entering Canada

The big day had arrived, maybe the second biggest on the trip. I had just completed a wonderful evening at the Camaray Motel in Oroville, nearly a model for what evenings in the little towns of my bicycle adventures should be. A few things stood out about last evening. The owners/managers of the motel were very interested in my trip. Their knowledge of the area was important, not only of the town but also of the upcoming route. Often I have to ask someone about needed information that I can't find otherwise. Clyde and Sandy certainly filled that bill. The motel was spotless. It was in a great location, and it was very quiet. The best motels are right on my route, especially at the end of a long day. This one was. Plenty of nearby options, and especially a grocery store, are always a plus. A super hot shower and a decent bed matter too. I got it all and was ready to leave the U.S. for about 20 days with hopes that I would find more motels like this.

This morning, the first thing I did was call Verizon and

set up the Travel Pass. It costs $5 a day to use their international calling plan. AT&T doesn't charge, or at least that is what I had been told. I was ready to ride into Canada but very apprehensive about what my next phone bill would look like. Remembering that my last bike journey into Canada was full of cell phone issues that never were solved, I was not confident, especially with the remote areas my travels would reach.

I pedaled the short four miles to the Canadian border customs area and took a few photos of where I would cross. The border was open 24/7 and I understood often had big delays. But on this early Saturday morning, I was next in line after just one car. In fact, I was first but pulled over to take a few photos. It took the car just 2-3 minutes to pass through, and the officer motioned for me to come forward. I did, not really sure what to expect. Things went sour quickly. I know I was smiling, because I almost always am. The customs officer was grim faced and started asking rapid-fire questions. He first asked if I had ever been to Canada before. I told him I had on several occasions but only one other time on the bike. He asked, "Where did you enter?" I told him that I had entered at Buffalo, and he quickly responded, "Sir, Buffalo is in your country!" I told him I knew that but I did enter at Buffalo and didn't remember the Canadian name for the crossing spot. This one was Osoyoos and I knew I wouldn't remember that either.

Rapidly, he started asking about fruit in my bags. I told

him about one banana, and before I got that out he said, "Do you have any firearms?" I said no, but obviously not fast enough because he said, "Sir, do you have any firearms in your bag?" I had had enough and told him, "Just give me time to answer the first question before you are firing another. There is no reason to get snippy!"

With that, the officer decided to show his authority. He told me to pull the bike over and enter at the next door; they were going to run a background check on me. I wondered why he didn't harass the woman in the car ahead of me this way.

I stood inside with my iPad, just in case I needed to have a picture of something, I guess. The jerk officer passed off my passport to another officer at the desk and went back outside, not to be seen again. Who would want to?

The new officer was quick to say, "Have you ever used any other names?" Without a joke, I just said no. Then the officer wanted to know what my journey was and where I was going. I noticed his name tag and read that he was Officer Williams. When he learned I was on my bike to Anchorage, he was all smiles and called up several versions of maps to discuss my route. We both started to smile, and suddenly I was getting great information. He turned his screen around for me to see and I showed him my planned MapQuest route.

Within minutes, Officer Williams had convinced me to alter my course and continue on B.C. 97 instead of a shorter but possibly more dangerous route. That was the same idea that Clyde Andrews at the Camaray Motel was promoting, so I decided to agree. They knew the roads; I did not. And I would still end up on the same far north roads later.

Officer Williams was really into it. He also suggested that I not follow the Cassiar Highway, a very remote section that would shorten the trip north by about a hundred miles. "There is nothing there, and supplies are hard to come by. I wouldn't do it," he said. Later I would learn that many cyclists struggle with the same question. The Cassiar or not? I decided to hold off until later on my own decision.

Pretty sure that Officer Williams didn't see me as much of a threat to Canada, I asked him if I could take his picture for the paper. He agreed and got up from behind his desk to do it. We shook hands and he gave my passport back. "You are free to go!" the officer said. He will get one of my books if I can figure out how to send it to him.

Back on the bike, I realized that there was a big British Columbia sign nearby, and I wanted a photo with it. As if on cue, a woman walked over and asked if she could take my picture. She told me that she had just taken a photo for another American going to Alaska, but he was in a truck. I got my photo and next stopped by to exchange some money at the duty-free shop. That went well, and soon I was pedaling north again on 97. I still wanted to stop in a visitor center and ask questions, get maps and other information.

The first visitor center at Osoyoos didn't open until 10

a.m. so I pedaled on. A long series of small towns was just ahead, but I decided to stop at the visitor center in Oliver, where Cait Wills helped me. She also called ahead to another visitor center in Kelowna to prepare more things she thought I would need. The British Columbia towns of Okanagan Falls, Kaleden, Pentiction, Summerland and Peachland finally led me to Westbank. Most of the riding was along Lake Okanagan, a large portion of that moderately challenging and into a wind. Some of the winds were fierce enough that I struggled to make headway. With 79 miles done, the first day in Canada was hard, but now done.

On Sunday, I would be back on B.C. 97 to head west through towns of Vernon, Falkland and Kamloops. I already knew that my AT&T phone was working, my iPad would not send emails and I had found a British Columbia map. The pricing here was crazy, with gas nearly $6 a gallon but sold in liters. McMuffins were well over $4, and most regular snacks were about double what they are at home. I felt a little lost and unprepared, with plenty of reading to do. Sundays were usually good, so I was optimistic about the coming day.

A good night at the Highland Motel in Falkland, B.C., provided some extra sleep. The morning went so well that I felt good about taking some extra time to try to get my iPad working. A stop at McDonald's in Kamloops would serve several purposes, but mostly to see if the high quality WiFi could send my stories, emails and photos. If not, my tech advisor back at home, Amanda Lewis, was going to work with me to see if we could figure out a workaround. My phone was still working with no issues, and I could talk with her while we tried some things. Nothing worked after an hour of trying. Although I had eaten while we tried those things, I knew that there was a long way to go, and burning an hour was hard to take. Amanda is a super tech expert, knowledgeable in plenty of things I am not. She had already set up my new iPad better than the folks at Verizon, so I had confidence. But with no solution, we were back to the drawing board. A certain level of anxiety had begun to build on this day, with the uncertainty of the connectivity and the long ride ahead.

Then I made a couple of mistakes. While I was in McDonald's, another customer sat across from me and listened to everything we were doing. For a solid hour, I wondered about his interest and why he didn't move on. Then he followed me outside and asked more about my ride. Colin introduced himself and said he very much wanted to do something similar himself, so I took time to answer his questions. Eventually, I had to go. Colin said, "Right up there is where you are going!" I saw this giant hill rising above the town, probably well over a mile away. To top it off, the wind had changed and I no longer had a tailwind.

The second mistake was made when I saw that a sign for B.C. 97 pointed toward an exit into town. I took it and later realized that it was probably a business exit of some kind. Traffic and lights were everywhere, and I was confused about how to get back to that big hill and the bypass. A mechanic told me the only way to do it now was to climb about 20 more blocks through town, one light at a time. It was now hot and so was I. Too many things weren't going right. I took time to stop at a convenience store and get a cold drink and a couple of candy bars. I needed energy and a lot of it. The day had turned south — not my direction, but my mood. There was much to do, but all I could think of was the need to get out of Kamloops, which was probably a nice town but I just couldn't appreciate it.

Finally out of town on the highest hill around, I started to get an occasional break from climbing, but the wind had become an issue. A directional change was battering me as the long climbing returned. I still had 40 miles to go, and the day was getting away from me. I didn't have enough food or water to stop out there to camp. Options only pointed to pushing through even after dark if need be.

With absolutely nothing worth seeing around, I was getting cold, and it rained a little bit. For the first time on the trip, I was miserable. My thoughts and energy were all focused on getting to Cache Creek. I was still 10 miles away and had just enough battery power in my phone to find an affordable motel. I locked up the Sundowner. The light was fading, and I was tired and ready to get this day over with.

Mercifully, the last couple of miles into town were mostly downhill. I stopped at a huge convenience store and loaded up on food and water before looking for my motel. The bags were so full, I thought items might fall out.

Near dark and without a working taillight, I didn't want to take time to talk with an adult skateboarder who came walking over with questions. But once again, I took time to answer them. He, too, wanted to do something similar and was interested in my route. Finally, with mosquitos getting active, I rode toward the motel. It had been the longest day of the trip and nearly the most miles at 98. I was physically wasted. It was the kind of day that had little to brag about. Still, one of my best memories from the first year of adventure cycling was a phone conversation with then-night editor Paris Goodnight at the Post. A similar day had occurred in Wyoming, and I had nothing but bad things to talk about. Paris said, "OK, so what were the good things that happened? There are always good things!" He was right, and I reached back to remember the wonderful morning ride that got me to Kamloops in time to try the possible solutions. So tired and so behind, I didn't worry about more, but I knew for sure that I was glad to have experienced this day. More good days were coming! And I had plenty of food, a hot shower and a good bed ahead. I was OK.

At this point, I had to write the updates on Pages, an Apple version of Word, AirDrop it to my phone and then send it to the paper that way. Nothing else worked. All this made my head hurt. We would keep working on solutions. For sure, I just wanted to deal with riding the bike, finding the best route and staying supplied with food and water.

After a very late night in not the nicest motel, where I got what I paid for, I was somehow up again and excited about today's ride. I knew when I stopped at the Sundowner that the outside didn't look well kept and much of it was probably filled with long-term residents. Some of the vehicles looked like they didn't get moved often. Two guys were sitting outside my door, but they weren't in the way when I rolled the bike in. I assumed I had talked to the owner when I called. She was so nice and sympathetic to the fact that I had miles to go. "Don't worry, I will have you a room!" she said. And the price was right, for sure.

Inside the room, I went around checking to see what worked, and nearly everything did. The room was stuffy, and I had to figure out how to turn on the air conditioner without any knobs. Having a multi-tool in my bag seemed the solution until I figured out the knobs probably had been removed to keep down the number of adjustments. I was able to turn it on and it worked, somewhat. There was a small kitchen in the room too, nothing that I would use, but I warmed more toward the room as the night went on. The shower was fantastic. Even with a lot of folks in residence, it had plenty of forceful, hot water. Back to my mantra on motel rooms: "I only really need it to sleep and will likely be here just a few hours." The WiFi worked fine, but I still had to use my longer process to submit the story.

Up early the next day, as always, I left the motel and

felt better. I was on the way to another day's adventure. At the intersection, I was initially confused on which way to go. Having consumed most of my large tonnage of food, I needed more and expected that the same store would have egg biscuits and someone good with directions. The wind was swirling, not much different from a few hours ago. I dreaded the likelihood that I would face it again.

Inside the store, I ordered a couple of egg and cheese muffins. The place was already busy, and a weathered guy was working the counter. I told him where I thought I was going, and he pointed back toward the same way that I had come last night. That couldn't be. Frankly, I never wanted to see that road again. So I pulled out the map and showed the guy, and he took a real interest this time. Nobody else was in line. "You want to go to Chasm, not Chase. You are on the right road," he said. Much relieved, I left the store headed out of town and one more time into the wind.

I had hoped to wait to eat the biscuits until I had made 10 miles or so, but with progress going slow, I stopped to eat after the first at two miles. Now going upward again on B.C. 97, I could see a long morning of challenges again. I climbed a mountain that took most of the morning and had only 25 miles by 11:30 a.m. At one point, I stopped to get a drink. When I tried to remount the bike and pedal into the wind, I couldn't move forward with all my weight applied. More prayer for strength and a lessening wind seemed to help, and eventually I was rewarded with a downhill into the town of Clinton.

Clinton had several interesting antique shops and two convenience or market-type stores. I took time to stop at both, beginning with another Petro Canada. The clerk was really nice but didn't know why her store had no crushed ice. Just not a thing up this way was my best opinion. With a couple of items from there, I headed on toward a Shell that served as a small grocery. It had been highly advertised as I entered town and did have some good things — lots of food and souvenir items, with clothes, hardware items and more. The clerk wanted to know about my ride. At both stores, the clerks told me the riding ahead was nowhere near as bad as I had just experienced. Never quite sure whether to believe these good tidings, I hoped for the best.

Right away, I had a huge hill to conquer, but the road was way more interesting. At the rest stop near the top of the hill, I met Raimo Laosma of Estonia. He was cycling from Fairbanks, Alaska, to Argentina and would take the year to do it. He had already completed many ultra-long trips and kept talking about them. He extolled the never-ending hills between here and Alaska. "Always up and down," he said. Raimo was the first long-distance cyclist I had met, and it sounded to me like this was his current life's work. One trip after another.

The morning was once again beautiful. The road ahead was part of the old stage route. Towns were named after the distance covered by the stage, and I enjoyed the opportunity to ride into history. Still cycling into a serious wind and experiencing a cold day, I would pass through Chasm and then 59 Mile House, 70 Mile House and 83 Mile House. Up and over Begbie Summit at 4,041 feet, the ground finally leveled out some. I met my first serious mosquitos of the trip, at one point able to see them ahead easily. They were large and black, and I had never seen mosquitos so active. Despite so many of them flying ahead, I was not bitten often. That was probably due to the sleeves and pants I had on, and maybe the wind too.

Many friends had told me about their experiences with the mosquitos in Alaska. I would have my own stories later, but this incident was a small sampling of the attacks to come. Lots of standing water was around, and I suppose that affected the size and volume of the persistent pests.

100 Mile House was the largest of the towns just ahead and, with the conditions, I was ready to look for a motel. Within the last 10 miles, light rain and pea-sized hail fell. I closed and buttoned up my bags, but the only real change came in wind direction. No longer just a headwind, it swirled some, but the intensity lessened with the heavier rain as I neared town. The temperature dropped, and I became colder with each mile. Late afternoon should have been full daylight, but the cloud layer and streetlights made the area look like early evening. I needed to find a room and get warm. In reading about the area during summer, I knew that cold and hot were both likely and I was ready.

After just 71 miles, I called two motels and found that they were full, but the Red Coach Inn was suggested as a possibility. With the rain still coming down, I rode there to take my chances. Another negotiation took place for the room rate, and I used some of my Canadian money to get a better price. Clearly once a grand motel, this one had seen its better days. My room was first-class, though, and I tested the heat right away. All my clothes had time to dry out, and a grocery nearby had plenty of good items to eat. "Let it rain," I said, while comfortable and out of the elements. I again had to focus on the problems involved with sending my update and photos to the Post. I looked forward to putting this problem in the rear-view mirror.

Early the next morning, I got a picture of the last stage-coach used by the B.C. Express. Now glassed-in at the motel and quite beautiful, it probably was the inspiration for the Red Coach Inn name. With the weather still wet and cloudy, I wanted to get a few things at a 7-Eleven on the way out of town. This chain had been good to me over the years, and this store was too. I noticed a rack of hats, some of them floppy hats meant to shield out the sun and slow down the rain. One with an adjustable cord to keep it tight to the head caught my eye. I tried it on and couldn't believe the price of just $9.99, so I soon had my primary hat for the rest of the trip. I would later be seen entering Alaska sporting this slightly grimy and less-new looking head covering. It was my first lasting purchase along the way and I loved it. Also at this 7-Eleven, using only a credit card wouldn't work because a card of normal thickness wouldn't register. The clerk handed everyone another card to bulk it up and we had to insert both at the same time. Once the transaction was complete, you just handed the extra card back. One guy laughed and said, "You don't come here often, do you?" I wondered how long this extra step had been required.

The wind and cold continued as I hit 108 Mile House, complete with a nice rest area and an amazing restored stagecoach stop that included lots of farm buildings. It was cold enough that I relished time out of the wind inside the rest stop. My mittens were keeping my hands warm, but just barely. Snow had been reported nearby, as I had occasionally been able to receive radio stations while in and out of the hillier sections. My thoughts were on Williams Lake ahead and taking time to call Verizon and Windstream for technical help.

Assured multiple times that all my devices would work, I had lost patience and needed to get more help from the companies involved. I felt behind all the time and less prepared than I should be for the next day's ride. Something had to give, and losing sleep as the only solution just wouldn't work.

I rode through Lac la Hache, both the lake and the little town, with several motels calling my name. Only because I was beaten back a little bit would I even consider stopping so early in the day, but that thought was pushed away. Occasional rain started to fall, with sections of less cloudy sky. I cheered for the warm sun to find me and soon it did. The suffering in the cold lessened and my mood improved. I was confident of being patient enough to get technical solutions later that day.

A long and well-done paving project just this side of Williams Lake afforded a great road to ride as I neared my stop for the afternoon. I could see the huge lake and a good portion of the lakeside road. A brief stop at the visitor center netted some info for the long ride ahead. A whole section on the Yukon and Alaska made me limit what I took, for weight purposes. The volunteer was extremely helpful, so I left with plenty to read.

My room for the evening was at the Valley View Motel, complete with a beautiful view of Williams Lake. Once in the room, I left the bike outside and settled in to start the calls for technical support. I began with Verizon and kept being transferred after I described my issues. Told often that the Travel Pass should work, I wondered if these folks had ever actually been in the less populated areas of British Columbia. I gave up on Verizon after an hour of being placed on hold too many times.

Two more hours with Windstream frustrated me to no end. I could see the beautiful day out the window, and I just sat there listening to reasons for transfer after transfer. After one more rant, a woman went to get the long-promised technical expert on the phone. In the revelation of the day, a laidback man came on the phone and said, "What can I do for you?" I explained the issues again, and he simply replied, "Sir, I don't know what these people have been telling you, but Windstream doesn't support email delivery in Canada. It won't work." The line disconnected, but I had my answer.

Glad that my AT&T phone was working and that I could still send email from it, I knew a little more than before and still dreaded what might happen as I cycled into more remote areas. Connectivity was likely to become even more complicated, and I wondered if there would be a point that would require me to get back into the U.S. before I could send updates.

I shut down everything and left to go to the McDonald's a mile down the road for some much-needed food. Egg McMuffins and some pastry specials perked up my mood.

Now I was on what is known as the Cariboo Trail for the stage line that began moving people and supplies in the area after gold was discovered nearby in 1861. It's also known as the British Columbia Gold Rush Trail. Mosquitos were becoming more active by the day, and occasional horseflies were joining my little ride. Exposed skin was at a minimum as long as the temperatures remained chilly.

I had seen no major wildlife in British Columbia, although bear-proof trash receptacles were becoming common. Moose warning signs now showed up on occasion. Blisters seemed to be developing on my feet, and I needed a little more sleep. There were lots of issues to address in the days ahead. A tailwind had to be coming soon; the odds were in my favor. Quesnel was the next decent town ahead. My destination for the day would be Prince George, the largest city in Northern British Columbia.

CHAPTER 5

To Kitwanga

With a decent night just passed in Prince George and the Bon Voyage Inn, I remembered Postmaster Barry Johnson saying that the terrain would smooth out a little north and west of this area. I wondered if that could be. The motel had its own attached restaurant and a convenience store on site. I had used the restaurant right away for a great veggie burger and a cool coupon deal this morning that let me get three items for breakfast. My choice was two huge muffins and a fruit cup. The convenience store was overpriced on most everything, but it had no competition. I just purchased some water and ice cream the night before and not much else. Two ice cream sandwiches for $4 were bearable, and they hit the spot.

I noticed that the motel price was high already and the motel tax was 18%. The Bon Voyage complex was about the last thing in town, and I asked the store clerk what I could expect going forward on this chilly and drizzly morning. He told me about a store about five miles west and said then there would be nothing for a long time.

The best news of the day was that, with all the troubles involving Windstream and Verizon so far, Amanda Lewis figured out a workaround that shows real promise. I already had a Gmail address but have never used it. Amanda set up a new one to see if I could send and receive on the iPad using Verizon and Gmail. I was amazed that it worked; she probably was not. Windstream had proved useless, except when fronted by another carrier on my cell phone.

With the temperature in the mid-40s and no wind, I rode northwest virtually alone. I didn't start off with long pants, but the chilly morning demanded them rather quickly. I stopped at that next store and got my two egg and cheese biscuits at the always-reasonable Petro Canada convenience store. Already this chain had earned my respect for reasonable pricing. A banana was 50 cents and it wasn't even close to being overripe. This particular store had fresh homemade pastries too. With a light rain starting to fall, the long pants and my rain jacket felt good. I went back inside with one more request. I had learned on previous trips to wrap my winter mittens in plastic bags to keep the rain out so my hands would stay cozy warm.

Headed into 50 miles of no supplies, I made sure to have enough. There was very little traffic. The chilly morning in this wooded area would be interesting, especially now that bear and cub signs were posted for the first time. I met a local cyclist out for a training ride who had seen eight bears in the last two weeks, and one appeared to be charging him until a tractor-trailer happened by.

The first town of the day was Vanderhoof, best remembered for a long downhill into town and only a moderate uphill to leave. It seldom works that way. Vanderhoof is also the geographical center of British Columbia. This little town was extra friendly, and I took the opportunity to reload my bags with food and water.

I had a tidbit of information on a lodge/motel ahead in Fort Fraser. Wayne Eller, a former Rowan County resident I might see the next day, helped me by calling ahead to line up the room at the Last Spike Motel with Ron and Vita Adair. Ron and Vita were lots of fun. I could have talked with them for a long time, but my other duties beckoned. I wanted to see if I could transmit my report and photos. Finally, I was quite hungry and the nearby Petro Canada had a recommended restaurant in it too.

Ron used to work with British Intelligence and was a huge President Trump fan. In fact, he was in the process of sending an email to the president and showed me what it was about. Vita was a journalist, and they run a motel whose main niche is as a hunting lodge.

Fort Fraser is where the symbolic last spike was driven to join up the last rails of the Grand Trunk Pacific Railway, connecting across Canada. Ron gave me a miniature spike to keep.

I unloaded some of the bag space into the very nice room

and rode down to the store/café. Told by more than one person to try the café, I went right away to check the menu. The café owner was working and asked what I would like. Taking a chance, I asked for an omelet. She agreed to make it and I was on cloud nine. I had a good day, was going to eat very well and my data back to the Post should transmit. I already knew that I had good WiFi in the motel, so I had a reasonable chance to get it done.

Besides the omelet and hash browns, I also picked up plenty of water, a breakfast pastry, a Mr. Big candy bar and an ice cream sandwich. I doubted that much of this would last the night. By the way, Mr. Big was my new favorite — super large, available at most stores and reasonably good to not get mushy in the heat.

I was getting close to halfway to Alaska after 81 miles today, still holding that 80-mile average. The more remote areas are coming along with more challenges. And the wildlife is just around the corner. All my writing and photos transmitted just fine tonight and it looks like we have that part going well. I have WiFi to use here but it is unlikely to be as available coming up.

Now that the rooms often have fans, I love to use them overnight. A very good female runner friend always travels with a fan. It might work for me too at another time. With space and weight as a premium, the fan idea wouldn't do well on the bike.

By the time I went to bed, I had washed out my cycling

shorts and hung them on a chair outside to dry. The wind was up again, and I hoped they would be dry when I woke up in the morning. The wind blew them off the chair overnight and did the same with a pair of socks.

When I got up, I dried the shorts on the fan, another great job for it. The socks wouldn't dry as quickly so I got another pair from my bag to wear, while hanging the damp pair from my tent to dry on the bike. On this whole trip, I never used a washer or dryer and didn't need to. The shorts and T-shirts, plus the socks, all washed out pretty well. And the Dri-Fit stuff usually dries quickly anyway.

Up on Sunday morning, excited again for another good day, I pedaled to Frasier Lake without even bothering to stop again at the wonderful Petro Canada store. Frasier Lake was a slightly bigger town with a hopping convenience store too. I got a couple of breakfast biscuits there plus some other things, talked with the clerk for a few minutes and then pedaled on through Endako, where little was happening.

I spotted a recumbent cyclist pulling a trailer and heading toward me. Since I hadn't seen anyone cycling for a few days, I looked forward to hearing the latest about what was ahead. German cyclist Alfred Zielinski from Cologne had started in Whitehorse, in the Yukon, and was on his way south to Vancouver. Not long after Alfred began his journey, he took the Cassiar Highway, the particularly remote and wildlife-abundant road that I would see soon. Alfred told me of his experience, which included a grizzly that had to be screened by a car for a getaway, and a black bear that didn't want to back off either. A big issue, too, was Alfred's shortage of water at times, partly due to lack of supply points. I paid close attention to everything he said, knowing that I could have the same experiences very soon.

Officer Williams at Canadian Customs had asked me to consider not doing the Cassiar, and at least one other friend from home who knew the area suggested it too. However, I had to do it. Otherwise, I would forever wonder what I had missed or if I could have done it. I resolved a long time ago to go for the experience when given the choice. Plus, the Cassiar was about 100 miles shorter than the alternative route, and I didn't need to add another day to my ride with July 12 looming closer each day.

I wished Alfred well and hoped he would be OK the rest of the way. He had encountered bears; I hadn't yet. But Alfred had survived a tough time and I would too.

Back to today's ride, I planned to call it a day at Burn's Lake and meet with Wayne Eller, even though I had only 59 miles. I would make it up, and the opportunities were coming soon. Wayne moved to this remote area of British Columbia two years ago and contacted me once I mentioned the route to Alaska in the paper. Wayne runs a ranch and trains and raises horses, all in an area with very cold winters. Even though his address was Burn's Lake, Wayne still had two ferry rides and a couple hours of driving to get to the actual town.

We had a wonderful Chinese dinner and talked about lots of things. It was one of Wayne's infrequent visits to town. He didn't want to forget something when he did come to town because the return trip was quite involved. I spent the night in the Burns Lake Motor Inn in a very comfortable room and totally enjoyed my visit.

Just one day away from halfway, I had been rained on twice today and for the third day in a row. The roads continued to get worse, and I hoped to make Smithers tomorrow. There was a good chance that I would shave 20 days' worth of beard growth there.

By my count, "halfway to Anchorage" day was here. It was 37 chilly degrees with not a speck of wind when I rode out of town. Wayne advised that the road would be better this morning, and it surely was. The morning ride was one of the best recently, with no serious climbing and ahead of pace. I rode through the small community of Decker Lake but had no reason to stop. On to Topley, I looked for the Grizzly Adams store that had been advertised on signs and billboards. Another store, probably a gift shop, was open. Grizzly's place was locked up tight well past the opening time.

I almost missed a big animal sighting and just happened to glance to the right as a huge deer was casually walking in the creek. Majestic with a big rack, it never looked toward me. Almost immediately, I saw two young female cyclists pedaling my way. Looking like they had just stepped out of a shower, these girls were smiling and seemed quite happy. Within minutes, two guys pedaled quickly to catch up, and frankly I would have too. I visited with David JB, Veise Laura, Jouet Remi and Datterac Noljwenn, all from France and riding from Anchorage to Patagonia. The group had planned the trip for several years and completing it would take another.

All of them spoke broken English. We used hand gestures to describe things and laughed our way through the conversation. The group didn't buy bear spray, but someone had given them some. At this point, I still had not seen a bear and thought I was missing out. It was interesting that I had the second half of my trip to go until reaching Anchorage and this group had started there. It seemed that we were making about the same pace.

Next came Houston, the only real town since Burn's Lake. Houston was small but had a large car dealership and a booming 7-Eleven. Cars were coming and going, with customers in and out and two cash registers running long lines. The busy store had jumbled shelves and about the dirtiest bathroom of the trip. Believe it not, I took time to help out a little in the bathroom. First time I have done that.

The railroad runs right through Houston and had lots of boxcars and flatbeds sitting on the rails, plus several diesel engines. At the very end of town came a steep climb up and over a river. For the first time in quite a while, I was seeing snowcapped summits again, all off to the west. Climbing the Hungry Hill Summit was rewarding, especially since I didn't know about it ahead of time. Beautiful green pastures with a smattering of white daisies were in the foreground as the beautiful peaks rose on the horizon.

Enjoyment from the pleasant riding slammed to a stop. Still 20 miles from Smithers, I pedaled onto a road that would become almost unbearable. Finished in a tar-and-gravel style of repaving, the road was not just rough; it also was quite dusty, even with slower traffic. Still on B.C. 16, I learned later that the road had been under construction for a long time, and drivers seemed interested in making up for past delays. The rush was beginning as I moved farther into the new paving. The dust was building, especially since a great number of the vehicles were trucks with multiple axles. I knew right away that the trucks had no interest in slowing, even as huge clouds of dust hung over the road. If only there had been more wind to blow it away. For this one day only, I prayed for more wind.

I began to taste the gravel dust in my mouth and closed my eyes as often as I could. I was miserable. I had no idea how much longer this would go on and wondered what I could do to help. The only reasonable solution would have been to pull a dirty T-shirt out of my bag and wrap it around my head, with only my eyes showing. Maybe I could have filtered the worst of it and still breathed enough to survive the rest of the road. I didn't do it but should have, as the gravel dust soon covered most of me.

With entrance into the small town of Telkwa, the new paving mercifully stopped. A much more pleasant ride continued on to Smithers. At least 10 motels were on hand and within four or five blocks. I had a conversation with a guy walking by who wanted to know about my bike ride, then he proceeded to tell me that I would be lucky to find a room in Smithers. I asked him why and if he could suggest a motel that might have budget prices. That word, "budget," seemed to turn him off. He said some of the motels we were looking at might cost $150-$200 a night. We clearly were not on the same page. I tried to end the conversation, but he kept talking. The paving project, the Canadian pipeline and a nearby railroad project all brought lots of people, and he said rooms were at a premium, jacking up the rates.

On the north end of town were three lesser motels. By that, I meant older, with less flashy parking lots and likely fewer amenities. I called one of them, got a high price and asked for a better one. Two teenagers seemed to be running the place, and they had no idea about discounts. I stopped at another, offered at exactly the same price. At the time, nearly 8 p.m., only a few cars were in the lots. I had enough food; I just wanted to get off my feet and bike saddle, get some sleep and get out of this "wanting an identity" town early tomorrow. I took the Mountain View Motel, settling for a room that was plain and old. It was large, which is usually a good thing, but I didn't care much this time. I sent my story and photos, ate everything I had, took a shower and went to bed. Enough for today! By the way, most of the view of the namesake beautiful mountain was blocked by obstructions of different types, including poorly kept bushes and trees. The good feeling associated with making 92 miles and surviving the major dust helped me count this day as one for progress. Later that night, I got the scourge of the downstairs tenant in a two-story motel. I envisioned a 400-pound person getting out of bed and lumbering around in the overhead room. It went on for about 15 minutes, during none of which I could sleep. Finally, I heard a door slam and the noise stopped.

The wild Cassiar Highway was just ahead, and I was nearing my last chance to back out. That wouldn't happen for me, but some cyclists would divert. I spent some time reading in Milepost on what to expect, now that the challenge was so close. Five or six days on short supplies was the thing that worried me most, especially after talking with Alfred, the German cyclist. I expect that if he had do-overs, Alfred would have chosen to avoid the challenging Cassiar. But Alfred did survive. So did the French quartet, and Julien too. No doubt, I would have stories to tell afterwards. The Cassiar was just one full day ahead!

Before leaving Smithers, I had worked out a plan to go to Hazelton's visitor center for more current information on the Cassiar. As another afterthought, I rode back to load my bags. The first nice place was the 7-Eleven store, and a good conversation soon ensued with the early morning clerk. He wanted to ride a bike on a long trip sometime, and I encouraged him to make that dream happen.

Riding back by the high-priced motels so early gave me a chance to see who really did have lots of vehicles on hand. None of the older places did, and I didn't especially care about the higher-priced places. All these much-in-demand rooms seemed like a well-planned scam.

Still on B.C. 16, I mostly had the road to myself as I left town with some mildly challenging riding — enough that my pace was dragging and so was I for some reason. Something miraculous happened as I glanced left. The most spectacular view of a snowcapped mountain and its own glacier lifted my morning tremendously. The view was all for me. Then I spotted the most exceptional rest area of the trip. With no one else around, I leaned the bike against a picnic table and checked out the surroundings. There just above me was the Bulkley-Nechako Glacier, and around me was the most modern rest area in a perfect place. What set this rest area apart from all the others, except one, was that the little buildings were new, very clean and amazingly had WiFi. Rest areas in Canada are not big buildings with multiple restrooms and plenty of water. Usually they consisted of small buildings that house a toilet similar to a portajohn, a window or two and the toilet paper racks. Nothing else and certainly no potable water. The floors are concrete, and usually the walls and floor look as if they are hosed off on occasion. The decision to place the facility at the best viewing site for this glacier was wonderful.

As the scenery improved with more mountains, some with snow and some without, the riding got more challenging. A few signs touted Moricetown ahead just as a spectacular river came into view. Lots of vehicles were pulling off the road for photos and I joined them.

The little crossroads community of Moricetown, part of an Indian reservation, intrigued me. The convenience store was well stocked with the usual items, plenty of Indian craft goods and some baked goods. In fact, the bakery truck was unloading as I walked in the front door. Some wonderful-looking blueberry muffins were just coming off the truck in three-packs. The cashier said the pack was $4.50, a great deal compared to the recent stores visited, so I grabbed a pack right away. With a few more things, I went outside to look around.

Not quite ready to get back on the bike and with some eating to do, I walked the bike across the street to where a beautiful and ancient looking baseball field sat. It had plywood fences all the way around and a weathered covered grandstand. I could only imagine the games that had been played here and those that I hoped still were being played. Two authentic-looking totem poles were also on the property. With no one else around, I enjoyed one of the blueberry muffins while envisioning this tribal gathering place and all the activities it must have seen.

Now cloudy skies seemed threatening. Back on the bike, I rode on toward the side-by-side towns of Hazelton and New Hazelton. I'm not sure why there was division between old and the new. I was glad to be close to the visitor center and my final sendoff toward the thrill and challenge of the Cassiar Highway. B.C. 16 was the main street for both towns. As one of the girls at the visitor center told me later, "There is only one road; you can't get lost."

Kimmi Fuller and Taylor Barr gave me plenty of information and maps for the Cassiar, plus some of the local lore. They also suggested that I load my bags with food from Hazelton before leaving. "The scenery gets better and the climbing isn't bad, but there are no other stores until you reach Kitwanga," Kimmi said. "So, plan on loading up here before you leave town, and then do the same at Kitwanga. The campground is a good one!"

I always imagine the towns ahead and what they will be like. My imagining is usually way off. Such was the case as I rode toward the teeth of the adventure. Taylor and Kimmi had done a great job of describing what I would find; they even called ahead to see if I could get bear spray. They thought I would need it, but not for the black bears. While black bears spooked and ran away, grizzlies could be aggressive. I asked if a 100-mile ride would be possible for the first day of the Cassiar, just so I could reach the next supply point. That was the solid plan as I left Hazelton and rode north.

Some of the most beautiful scenery to date made this portion of the ride wonderful. Another perfect and almost windless day added to my enjoyment. I rode, full of thought and anticipation on one of those signature days that make these ventures so worth doing. Always hard to complete, but just flat out worth it!

Not far from the terminus of my ride on B.C. 16, I saw a school bus slowing ahead of me. The female driver stopped in the road and leaned out her window to say that a black bear and two cubs were just ahead and to be careful. I was going to see bears, finally! A tingle of excitement kicked in as I rode forward. Would It be dangerous?

The bear family was eating off the side of the road, exactly as the bus driver described. I made my photos from 50-60 feet away, and eventually they just wandered on. My first bear encounter had come and gone. Now it was time to head to Kitwanga and chase the real adventure. After some great river views and a few odd looks from the natives in the area, I found the beginning of B.C. 37 and the long-awaited Cassiar Highway. I also saw a big sign that said, "North to Alaska" and expected a photo opportunity there. It never happened and here's why.

I went into the Petro Canada store at the junction of 37 and 16, ready to buy my bear spray. Already assured by the girls that the grocery in Kitwanga was the place to get supplies, I didn't plan to buy anything else, although a few questions were on my mind. Two defining things happened quickly. I asked the owner seated at the cash register about the bear spray. His response was, "No, we don't have it, but the grocery in Kitwanga does." I told him about the girls at the visitor center calling ahead to see if he carried it and he didn't recall anything similar. My calmness from the afternoon went away in the next moment when the owner called a customer's name nearby and asked, "Hey, Ben, this guy is going to ride the Cassiar toward Alaska; do you think he needs bear spray?"

In one of the most memorable and unsettling moments from the whole ride, this Buffalo Bill-looking character said, "Hell no, you don't need bear spray! You need the biggest pistol you can find! Those bear ain't going to stop for bear spray! Hell, are you on a bicycle? You must be a stupid son of a bitch to think you can ride that road on a bicycle! It ain't safe, I tell you!"

I will admit to being a little shaken. Not sure what to say, I could only reply, "Yes sir, I am going to ride the road on a bicycle, been planning it for quite a while!" Ben had a wild look in his eyes, probably not totally to do with bear, but he had my attention. All this took only a few minutes.

I asked the owner again about the grocery. He said, "Well you better hurry! They close in 10 minutes and it's three miles away." I told him I couldn't get that far in 10 minutes. "Sure you can, I have a brother-in-law who walks it every day in 10 minutes," he said. "You got a bicycle!" So I asked him to call ahead and ask them to wait on me, and I would push it as hard as I could. Probably smiling to himself, the owner added: "And it is nearly all uphill!" I asked for directions. "Just go, you can't miss it!" he said. "There is just one road."

The calamity didn't end there. I rode away, pushing as hard as my "getting stronger every day" legs would allow. About a mile into the rapid ascent, I saw a guy running toward me, wide-eyed and in an obvious hurry. I stopped to ask, "Is the grocery store up here?" He replied as he kept running, "Yes, but there is a bear just ahead!" What kind of world was I entering? I never saw that bear.

About three miles in, the road leveled considerably, and a sign pointed toward Kitwanga. So there was a second road! I took it and quickly found the grocery, a very modern looking place with surroundings that didn't fit. Most everything else looked used up and rundown, but I saw a figure inside the store. I entered and asked if he had received a call about me. The man, named Thys, told me he had, and he pointed toward a well-stocked, medium-sized grocery. Without realizing what had happened, I experienced a signature moment of my ride. I found out the store not only closed at 5 p.m., but it also didn't open until 9 a.m., simply way too late for me to hang around to begin my ride the next morning.

The clerk went with me and we collected things I thought I needed, all in just a few minutes — ice cream, cookies, Pop-Tarts, a sandwich, chips, water, fruit and more. The clerk offered a couple of muffins. "I will donate these!" Satisfied that I had enough, he said, "I am not sure the checkout register will work after closing. I have never done this." It did work, and I ended up with $32 worth of groceries and very glad to spend it. I counted myself lucky to complete this stroke of good fortune. What if I had dallied with the bear or river photos, or Buffalo Bill?

Lesser points of discussion soon came up as I prepared to leave and see if all the new items would fit in my bags for the ride to the campground. Thys said that many of the cyclists who came through liked to sleep at the park, where it was free. I asked what the campground cost but was reasonably sure that the fee would be fine. Thys didn't know. I said I need WiFi and maybe a shower, although that subject would become way less important for the rest of the ride. I asked about the Cassiar itself, and he said, "It might have some gravel sections, depending on construction, and it is hilly. You'll see wildlife for sure!"

That last statement reminded me to ask about the bear spray. Yes, the store had it at a cost of $50 a can. Leaning toward not buying it, I asked, "Do I need it?" Thys said, "I have lived here for 30 years and never needed it. Just give them their space and you will be fine!"

Enough questions asked, I just had one more. Can you point me toward the campground?

I rode with an overloaded bike toward another road and the bottom of a hill. The Cassiar RV Park was everything that the rest of the town was not — well kept, attractive and safe enough for a night in this crazy place. I pedaled in with a full bike load and went right to the office. The comical campground owner wanted to know all about my plan and was in no hurry. Half a dozen campsites were already filled, and he gave me the choice of most of what was left in a huge shaded area. I asked about WiFi and got the typical campground response: "Yes, I have it and it works good here near the office and at the gazebo. Everywhere else is spotty. You can camp near the gazebo if you want or even use the gazebo to sleep; it's not going to rain. That will be $20 for the night." He even had a meager ice cream supply, which was on my mind for later, but I never returned due to the poor flavor selection.

I took the gazebo and planned to figure out how to just put my sleeping bag down and not mess with the tent. I spread my food out on the gazebo picnic bench and started to chow down, hoping to complete my daily reporting. The daylight was likely to last quite a while, but I needed to sleep in preparation for an early start. A storm cloud began to show itself.

Still with plenty to do, I knew that the next supply point was about 100 miles away. While eating, I rearranged my bags, pretty sure with water refills at the campground that I would have what I needed to make it. In all likelihood, I would eat most of the things I bought tonight and leave the other things in the bag. Sure that a shower wouldn't happen, I didn't plan to wash anything, so my extra clothes and tools took their usual place with the emergency Pop-Tarts in what I called the outside bag, the one to my right as I rode. I always dismounted to the left and therefore kept my food and water in the inside, or left hand bag, making it quicker to grab. In fact, I didn't often totally button that bag down unless rain was coming.

Speaking of rain, it began to fall heavy enough that I didn't want anything not waterproof out in it. The space in the gazebo easily held all my gear, and I decided to type away on my update while the rain fell. Just far enough from the office to lose connection, I had to walk my iPad toward it to reconnect and then happily sat typing while the light rain fell.

I was content to think of sleeping in the unscreened gazebo. The idea seemed perfect until the rain stopped and the mosquitos started. I resolved to set up the tent even though taking it down in the morning would probably render a wet tent and add 15 minutes. I hadn't had a lot of issues yet with the mosquitos, but those on hand were already calling ahead to tell their buddies to get ready. This skinny cyclist was about to attack the Cassiar! Before me lay 450 miles of rugged terrain, no cell coverage, little chance of supply and plenty of wild animals. We should know soon if I needed that bear spray!

CHAPTER 6

The Cassiar Highway (B.C. 37)

My first night on the Cassiar, spent at the campground in Kitwanga, had a little drama. After I decided to put up the tent, a car pulled into the spot I had picked out before I decided to use the gazebo. A man and woman got out and tied their dog to a stake. The dog did pretty well to start, as long as it was daylight. I didn't think much about it until some time in the night when I heard something rustling around in the woods. The dog started to bark, occasionally growled, and eventually calmed down. Then the rustling came back and so did the barking. I had lost my flashlight early in the ride, in fact on the first night into Canada. A small woven bag was stolen, or I lost it somehow. Either way, my only light was in that bag. Now with the light gone, I couldn't shine it toward the rustling to see if the campground had a visitor.

Since my cell phone had no service even before Kitwanga and the start of the Cassiar, I hadn't worried about putting it in the tent. The light on my watch didn't work, so I couldn't figure out what time it was when the barking was going on. With first light, I got up and began packing to go. I found my phone and I was early, but a half hour to the good on this day would be a plus. There was a long and challenging road ahead.

With no breeze following the drizzly evening, the mosquitos had ownership of the place. Because of them, I packed as fast as possible. The wet tent would need drying out later, if possible, but hustling to leave the mosquito-infested area was all I thought about. With a clear morning, broad daylight was in place by 5:30 a.m. Three blocks from the campground finally seemed to be enough to leave most of the biting bastards behind.

According to Thys at the grocery store, I could expect a gradual climb in the beginning of the Cassiar, and that is exactly what I got. Even though B.C. 37 is still considered a highway, initially I saw a vehicle about every 10 minutes. That rate gradually picked up, but not by much. I seldom saw two vehicles at the same time.

I was on edge, looking for bears. Every cyclist I had seen so far had taken the Cassiar, and all of them saw plenty. They saw other wildlife too, so my eyes were wide open. My first bear sighting was one just in the grass, and he appeared to be really small, possibly even a cub. On this morning, nature's scenery was not at its best — just scrub trees and bushes. So the lookout for bear lifted things.

Another bear walked across the road far ahead, as much

as a quarter mile. It was gone when I got there. Two more were close together and chose to run as soon as they saw me. If I stopped, mosquitos quickly found me. Big horse-flies and little black ones kept flying around me all afternoon, but they didn't bite until late afternoon. The wind seemed to drive off the mosquitos, but it didn't bother the bigger flies at all.

A small thunderstorm finally caught up from behind, and then a serious one came at me from the front. I didn't worry about buttoning down the bags at first, but when the last one joined in with plenty of lightning, I tried to keep everything as dry as possible. Both my panniers, the bags in the back, and the handlebar bag are waterproof, but only if the clamps on both sides are securely buttoned. In dry conditions, I often just button down one side to have more room. After stopping at a grocery or once when hauling a small watermelon, I often couldn't hook either side. I sometimes piled the food high, but it still didn't come out unless bumps or curbs were in play.

Two hours of rain, some of it incredibly heavy, kept pounding down, and the temperature dropped. Any bears probably ran for cover too. Thinking back, this was the most miserable I was on the trip for several reasons. The temperature dropped so much that the rain and wind made it feel like the 30s or 40s. My hands were barely functioning already. Cars passing often sprayed me with more water, although I don't think they had much of an option. Standing water was everywhere. Slightly lighter spots would some-times show up in the sky, and I would envision them head-ing my way. Then the heavier clouds covered over those possible weather breaks, along with my attempts to lighten the mood. I was freezing and occasionally shivering even though I was pedaling through this as fast as possible.

A major bridge construction project was in progress and evidently had just been suspended because of the weather. I had a long steep climb to make, part of it on wet wooden boards and huge sheets of steel. Arriving at the top of the hill without issues was a big win, but I was so cold that it was hard to take time to be appreciative.

Finally, as the rain backed off from a downpour, a few motorcycles and cars came by on their way to where they needed to go. The motorcycle riders often waved, as they probably better understood my pain than those in the cars. Those on the motorcycles were likely wet and a little chilly too.

I doubled my prayers, almost constant now, for the sun to break through. If it did, I just knew that warmth and some level of comfort would come. Finally, I did get sun and an ever-brightening horizon ahead. Ready to make the Meziadin Junction, I had no idea what to expect. The miles were winding down to what might be a town or might not.

After spotting a sign for camping off to my left, I saw a couple walking downhill and away from the road in that direction. I stopped to talk for a little bit and mosquitos attacked. The couple was camping in the small campground, and my first question was whether this held the only amenities in the area. I knew camping was available and there was supposed to be a supply point too. The walkers didn't know of any place for supplies, but I had already seen a sign pointing toward lodging ahead. Still not having gained any knowledge pertaining to the area, I let them go on and began to ride on in hopes of losing the mosquitos, as much as anything. The rain and still air must have been inviting to them. I was close to my limit for the day at almost 96 miles.

Expecting a little community, I found a convenience store, a restaurant and a huge area that looked like a bunch of mobile homes jammed together in a semi-permanent way. Riding toward the junction became a severe uphill. When it became even steeper to reach the gravel parking area for all this, I got off the bike and walked. So what if the mosquitos came back? Mercifully, they didn't.

I leaned the bike outside the store, looked around at the odd setting and walked up the steep steps to go inside for more answers. With the mosquitos out, and flies too, I decided to ask about the sign for lodging and at the very least get a few answers on what was going on here. The store looked mostly new and probably about the same age as the separate restaurant.

The young store clerk had a couple of customers, but nothing for the amount of trucks and cars that were parked nearby. Maybe the people were in the restaurant or the mobile home area. I asked the young woman, "What is this place? What is going on here? And do you have lodging? There was a sign just back down the road." That was a lot of questions for sure, but her answers would certainly set the tone for the night ahead.

Turned out that the whole complex was a work camp, and a huge number of workers were housed and fed here. I never heard where they were working but knew that lots of construction must be involved because of the vehicles and clothing. Interestingly, lots of women were here too. Lodging was available, but nobody else seemed interested in it. In fact, there were no other cars passing by. The time was about 7 p.m., closing time for the restaurant. It turned out the same woman ran the restaurant and the lodging. I asked about the price and was told that the woman was at the restaurant and would help me. I just needed to talk to her. The clerk said, "She is over at the restaurant cleaning up and I will let her know you are coming." Didn't sound like there was much of a demand for my type of lodging.

After several trips back and from the convenience store, I finally got Lori, the manager, to open the door to the restaurant. She told me about the accommodations. I would have a small room with a bed, a TV and a chair. Showers and bathrooms were spaced throughout the facility and were first come, first served. The price was OK, at $68. She said there was food in the store and the restaurant would open the next morning at 5:30 a.m. I told Lori that I needed to put my bike in the room and asked if that was OK. She said, "Not a problem, if you can find room to get it in there." This was developing as its own adventure.

I paid, received a key and was instructed to use the wooden steps nearby to enter the facility. I asked Lori who was housed here. "It's a work camp. People live here because it's too far to commute daily," she said. Nothing more. I left it at that.

Outside, several men and women were smoking near the closest set of steps and door. As they saw me coming, I was surprised that several offered to help lift the bike up the steps. I thanked them and one of the women showed me where my room was. The long hallways were frigid, with air conditioning on full throttle. I was still wet and now even colder.

What I found in the room was a small bed, a shelf and a few drawers, a mirror and sink, a window, a wooden chair and not much else. A floor vent was pouring out more cold air. As I wedged the bike in and thanked the woman, I saw that there was no TV. I asked about that and she said, "There is supposed to be one, and I will call so that somebody brings you one." Never saw that somebody or the TV, but I didn't need it.

Back to the store, I bought from a very small inventory just enough at super high prices to get through the night. Back in my room, I had three thoughts: Eat, do my reports on the sketchy WiFi and stifle the source of that cold air. I had two small towels in the room and threw one of them over the floor vent. Next I was amazed to find a wall thermostat, which offered a heat selection. I flipped the switch and the air gradually switched to a moderate cool, with the heat not able to override the force of the incoming cold air. Definitely, this was an improvement. It was still too cold to even think about going for a shower.

The night passed with little incident. The person in the next room had set an alarm for 4 a.m. and must have hit snooze every five minutes for more than an hour. It quit just before I was packed and ready to go, hoping to grab some food before leaving for an even worse segment of the Cassiar.

Turned out that the restaurant had opened at 5 a.m., but it was only for the work camp workers. The cook told me to wait until 7 a.m. and other outsiders would come in. I explained that I was on a bicycle with a long ride ahead and needed to get going. Was there anything that I could get? She pointed to a rack of prepared snacks and told me to take all I wanted. She gave me a price of $1.25 each. Apparently all the main workers were already out or she had plenty to cover her needs. I picked out eight things and paid her. I had 64 miles to go to another supply point, and the terrain was going to be challenging. The little convenience store was not yet open, but those snacks could be spaced out to make the distance. Loading up again later would keep me going until that evening. Just 64 miles was not enough for today; I had to keep moving. Tonight would be a stealth camping night. The level of adventure was ramping up.

I rode away from the work camp and realized that there was nothing else at Meziadin Junction. I started back uphill, and the first significant sign said, "Uphill for the next 20 kilometers." That one hit me in the gut. The mosquitos were already active and after me as I pedaled slowly along. I imagined a terrible morning.

The area felt like a damp jungle from the rain the previous evening. I began to see bear scat regularly in the road and tracks along the dirt edges too. The first bear saw me after just a mile and jumped in a tree. Only a few work trucks were driving by in probably the most remote section yet. Flies joined the mosquitos on this calm morning. My pedaling speed was down, as moderate hill after hill came at me. The king hill of the morning was more than a mile long, straight ahead and nothing but up at a steep grade, the first of its kind. None of the scenery in this area was special, or if it was, I couldn't see it for the low hanging jungle around me. The hills got worse, and the highlight was a short visit with a road crew out measuring for pothole repair. All of them were young and friendly. I asked what to expect ahead. The leader frowned and said, "A lot more like you have already ridden, all the way to Bell II." At least the jungle-like canopy had opened up and finally disappeared. So had the bear scat.

On this morning, I would have been pressed to find the

good things that copy editor Paris Goodnight reminded me about. Still, there was lots of day ahead and I was more than excited to see a nice rest area with several cars. Had I slipped so low on this morning that this was the bright spot?

I rolled into the parking area and almost immediately struck up a conversation with a pleasant woman who was driving her pickup along the same route as I was riding. She was sleeping in the back of the truck each night, and we talked about some of the things we both had seen and expected ahead. She showed me a very detailed list of the camping and parks ahead. This was a bright spot because I had not seen this list before. She had resolved to make one park about 60 miles on ahead, and I was a little disappointed to not have the ability to get that far. I did say, "Do you think the Cassiar will continue this challenging?" She replied, "I expect it will get worse, don't you? After all, we're going to Alaska." I thought briefly about trying to make those 60 miles anyway, but my total for the day would have been approaching 130, and that just wasn't possible.

My near-term goal for the day was Bell II, and I had no idea what that even was except a source for heli-skiing. It had a much-needed store and was just a few miles ahead. I had arrived at what they termed the Bell II Lodge. With camping on site and a motel, plus gas and diesel, this was a stop for almost everybody driving by. I had to as well, with my water bottles way down. Those wonderful snacks from the restaurant this morning had been my savior so far.

With little else in my bags, I had rationed them out. Carrot cake and a treat called Cherry Yum Yum were my favorites. There were scones too, a little smaller than I would later get, but I kicked myself for not buying double of everything after seeing the real truth of Bell II.

I parked the bike amid a huge swarm of persistent mosquitos, at that time the worst I had seen. Inside initially was a pleasant guy at the cash register who asked if I was riding a bike. I told him I was and my goal was Anchorage. I had picked out a few things from an area probably smaller than my den, more disappointed each time I looked at a price. The large water was $4.45, a price that will probably be remembered for years. Little cookie and chip bags were super high, and I just couldn't find much that I could make myself buy. In a surprise, the clerk said, "I would like to give you a bowl of soup. It is worth $10 and the last cyclist through paid ahead for the next one." The soup was coconut something and my lack of interest probably tipped him off that I have never liked coconut anything. I thanked him profusely and asked him to give it to the next cyclist. With that, I went outside and talked briefly to one of the resort workers. He told me that if I didn't like the price to camp, he could suggest some free places on up the road. I told him that I had to keep going. Later I wondered how much they would charge to camp.

As I was about to leave, another worker, female this time, walked over and asked about my bike ride. She seemed in no hurry, even though the mosquitos swarmed us. While she was talking, I decided to go back and bite the bullet for another high-priced water and a couple of snacks. There would be nothing else ahead for the rest of the day.

Back inside, the manager or owner or clearly someone in authority had replaced the nice guy at the register. I bought the other items and asked, "Can I use your WiFi? It's probably a long time until I will have a chance again to check messages." Her response was to point toward a sign that showed $6 for a half hour and $12 for an hour. I said, "I just bought over $20 of items. Do I still have to pay?" Her response was simply, "I can't give out free internet to anybody!" Nor a good price on much-needed water, I thought. The entire length of the Cassiar Highway had no service from Verizon or AT&T at any time.

One of the helicopters was flying as I left. The male worker said the resort owned several of the nearby mountain tops and would take skiers to multiple mountains during the winter to drop out of the helicopter to start their ski runs. Those mountains were all gloriously green now, with not a hint of snow.

Back on the road, I crossed over a small steel bridge to find the road had leveled out. For the rest of the day, I got one of those good things: another 20 miles without a significant hill! I saw four more black bears, one of which spooked me a little since he was standing in a curve. Yes, standing and staring at me, apparently not with any thought of running. The last portion of the ride had a couple of climbs but nothing as bad as the long morning.

During the morning, I had met Julie and Brian Harrell of Fort St. John, B.C., on their vacation while driving this same highway. Brian told me the Cassiar was nothing more than a long logging road that was eventually fixed up and paved over. Riding then under clouds and without wind, I began to notice something that would become routine. British Columbia, the Yukon and Alaska offered lots of what were termed pullouts. Just a gravel parking spot of varying size, some large and some super small. I noticed that campers and RVs would often set up overnight on them. I thought of doing the same.

The place where I chose to call it a day was near the Bob Quinn Rest Area, the Bob Quinn Lake and Bob Quinn Airstrip. Bob must have been a heck of a guy. A large sign prohibited camping, so I talked with another traveler who asked me where I planned to camp. He was in a pickup with a nice camper. I told him I would find a place out near the airstrip and get out of sight. I did just that, next to the fuel storage area and surrounded by huge mosquitos. For yet another time, I set up the tent as fast as I could, grabbed what I needed and dove in. I didn't come back out until early the next morning. The mosquitos settled on the screen to wait all night! I wrote my report, saved it and slept pretty well.

I was in the wilderness now. With no connectivity, I had to hold the updates and photos until I could send them later. Power to charge the phone and iPad were not a problem at all because the iPad uses very little and the two solar chargers I carried could easily charge the phone a couple of times. I was still probably at least three days away from any chance of cell coverage.

While lying in my tent that morning, I watched the mosquitos waiting to greet me once I ventured outside. Plenty of bites to my legs made me hustle to pack up the tent and get out on the road. Never having been bitten so much over such a short time did make me wonder if getting a spray would be OK this once. I just couldn't do it, at least not yet.

With 64 miles ahead to Tatogga, British Columbia, I pedaled on, knowing that supply was within reach again. Reports said the community had a good restaurant, a gas and fuel stop and flying service for airplane sightseeing. The hills kept coming, but by now it would be the rare time that hills didn't dominate the landscape.

At a campground near the road, I stopped briefly to see if there was WiFi. No sign of any, but I met Mike Miron of Port Huron, Michigan. Mike was taking a rest day after cycling from the Arctic Circle and developing spoke issues. He was on the way to Montana and would stop at the first bike shop, which appeared to be in Prince George. Spokes out of adjustment make the tire wobbly and out of round.

I met two brothers from Belgium, Julien and Frederic Gailliard, who were taking another great trip. They were riding to New York City from Anchorage. We shared the usual stuff about roads, animals, challenges and time of trip. I told them I had to be in Anchorage on the evening of July 12. Both asked why and looked at their trip computers, finally concluding that it was just about impossible to do unless I could ride 100 miles a day. That "impossible" word has always been a big motivator to me. I knew, even while the conversation was going on, that I would make it. If needed, I would ride through the night to make up miles. I had promised to be in Anchorage by that day. Just simply, I would be.

We had a wonderful and much deeper conversation than is usually shared by cyclists on these long-distance rides. We talked about the beauty of this road and questioned the lack of everything and the extremely high price of what they did have for sale. I knew these brothers would have a great time as they rode east. Chances were good for lots of tailwinds.

The brothers told me about a restaurant in Tatogga with reasonably priced food, free WiFi and nice people. They suggested that I stop to eat and use the WiFi. As we wished each other safe travels, I liked the idea of stopping to eat as an excuse to send my update and photos to the Post.

Just about 10 miles ahead was Tatogga, so I stopped to do those planned things. Since I could be inside for a while, I took my wet tent out of the bag, spread it in the sun and hung part of it over the bike. The tent had been in some form of damp or wet since very early in the journey, and

I was going to use it tonight. A dry tent would weigh less and be less moldy smelling. This one had that odor but had maintained its usefulness for lots of miles, states and adventures.

I went inside and saw pictures of all the breakfast items. It was my bad luck to be just a little late and have to order other things. I didn't want a meat sandwich, so I ordered French fries, two muffins and four cookies. I got the fries right away, a huge dinner plate full, and worked on them while I answered messages and sent my information. The muffins and cookies never came, nor did I get a bill. The lone woman working behind the counter was hustling and had a good crowd going, but I needed to be on the road. I walked up and asked to get the other stuff and she started on it. The muffins and cookies were frozen, so she asked, "Do you want me to warm them or just let them defrost as you ride!" "How about a little of both, just in case I want to eat some right away?" was my answer, but then I said, "They will defrost fine." I paid my bill, a very small one, packed my tent and rode on. A nice stop!

While there, I kept seeing cyclists coming in for water and talking about their lunch and dinner. When I left, they were sitting on the porch. Four of them, with all the best equipment, looked to be brand new at this kind of thing. This must be the group of four that the Belgium brothers told me about. They never moved from the time the brothers got there until I left, probably about three hours. I heard later that they got back on the road but I never saw them again. A particularly rough patch of climbing greeted them and me just past Tatogga. Maybe their long delay was a planning session or hope that the hills ahead would level out.

Up and down I went for a few miles. Then the road settled for a while as I entered Iskut, with a bunch of houses and one of the best community stores I had seen on the trip. It was clear that this store was the only one in town, and it was busy. I was able to load my bags with all kinds of good things in anticipation of late evening riding and some wilderness camping shortly thereafter.

While I was at the store, three motorcycle riders seemed to have issues; they kept saying, "What if … and maybe we can..." I never heard what the issues were, but I knew they were talking about another rider. As I rode away, there was a stretch of flat road with a long embankment down my side, with no guard rails. I didn't think much of it until I looked down and saw another motorcycle matching those I had seen at the store, lying at the bottom of a 40-50 foot drop-off. Guess that is where the other rider had a problem. The original three riders eventually blew by me and raced on ahead.

This had already been a big day for wildlife. I had seen three more black bears, my first lynx ever, a fox and two big beavers. After another huge late day climb out of the area past Iskut, I found myself on a high ridge with some great views and mostly flat to downhill riding. I saw an old sign with lodging listed three miles ahead and wondered if it was still there. It was not, and I began to think about finding a place to set up my tent. Those little pullouts were coming quite often, and I began to size them up for a camping location.

I was hungry. I pulled off at one pullout and looked around for a good tent spot while eating two bananas. I found lots of bear scat, fresh enough that I decided to do two things. First was to eat the last banana and leave all the peelings at this location. The second was to throw my stuff back on the bike and look for a better place. The next two pullouts were not significantly better, so I rode on. Past another hill, I decided to find something soon. The sun was getting low and I had a story to write. Near the top of a hill was a driveway with some trees next to it. I rolled the bike among the trees and saw only a small amount of scat. I set up the tent and quickly got some stuff inside, including a little more food for the evening. Then, for the only time on the trip, I walked the rest of my food on down the road and hid it.

Several things had become constant by this time. The emergency Pop-Tarts were always in my non-food bag and were the first thing to be replaced. Big downhills are not a source of joy. On this trip, a big uphill was just around the next corner. And wet bear tracks, usually from the dew, were common on the pavement early in the morning. In the most bear-populated areas, tracks in the dirt along the road were easy to see. The size of some of these tracks made me open my eyes a little wider.

My biggest concern was that friends, old and new, were sending me messages, and I was doing a poor job of answering them in a timely manner. I couldn't wait to get regular communication going again. A total of 78 miles was hard earned today.

The night went well, with no bears, and my food was still there when I went for it. The only surprise was that cars used the dirt road several times during the night. And they drove fast. Each time a vehicle came by, I woke up and waited to hear if someone got out and wanted to know who was camping. I heard a few heavy trucks on the highway, but all in all, I got some sleep. Not enough, but much-needed sleep.

I had seen several motels but not at the right places on my journey. I would have spent a little more money than normal just to get one in the right location, but there were "miles to go before I sleep" every day.

Packed up and on the bike early, I had one of those Tatogga muffins and wanted another. They were all gone, and I had to make it to Dease Lake, the last town with food on the Cassiar Highway. I had some other snacks, not many, but the Pop-Tarts were ready just in case.

On what became a drizzly early morning, I had to climb the highest point on the Cassiar, an oddly named challenge called the Gnat Pass. It took 20 linear miles to crest it, and once over the top, 12 miles of steady downhill to reach Dease Lake. As poor of a supply stop as Bell II had been, Dease Lake was about as opposite as can be. I described it to another cyclist later, and he decided on the spot to take a rest day there.

In the friendly downtown, the first words I heard were "Welcome to Dease Lake. It is great to have you here!" A guy headed out to his car took time to stop and say that, registering pretty high on my cool greetings list for the trip. I asked about WiFi and was directed back south for just a block to Northern Lights College, where the whole community had free access. After a couple of small food purchases from pleasant people at the store, I pedaled back south a long block to send in my latest work.

I couldn't get on the WiFi on my first try, and Tetreau Gueve offered to help. He made it work and we hit it off right away. We talked about my ride and how he had ended up in Dease Lake. That was quite a story, with some laughter, luck and hard knocks but a wonderful end result.

My first moose sighting came late that same afternoon, a lone moose on a casual stroll across the road and into the woods. No more bears showed themselves, and I felt confident about finding a place to sleep. Originally I planned to make close to 100 miles, if possible, to a park with camping, but I didn't make it and gave up with darkness nearing. My 80 miles had been a good day. Just as I started to find my camping site, I met more good people who added more to the good day.

Pierre was heading south and hoped to make South America. He was from France and was doing a documentary on the whole trip. He wanted to make the end of a lake I had just passed, and I just needed to find a good place.

I spotted a camper, a couple walking their dog and another big gravel pullout. It looked like a good place and maybe I would have company. The folks in the truck were just leaving, heading on to the same lake just to the south. Elton was the man, and we talked a little about why this would be a good campsite. They loaded me up with an apple, ice, water and Cokes. I waved as they drove away.

My tent took only minutes to set up in a hidden area, just as the mosquitos found me again. It didn't take long to dive into the tent and hope for an early completed update. I ate and wrote, already struggling with the need for good sleep. I left some of my stuff uncovered on the bike, thinking there would be no rain overnight. I was behind on planning and not as organized as I hoped to be at this point.

I awoke early, just as the rain came. And then the wind. I hadn't staked the tent down. It was a perfect night at dusk, and I had not experienced wind at all during the recent overnights. The wind got up enough that I had to hold the tent in place from inside. Within 10 minutes, both the wind and rain were gone. The mosquitos and I began the usual packing routine.

All the miles on the Cassiar Highway had been marked in 5K segments of 3.1 miles. Those 5K markers were great goals and I loved passing them. Missing my egg and cheese biscuits, cell service and most everything that makes these trips work, I was now a very long day from reaching the end of the highway and the Yukon. I was ready, with 110 miles ahead my goal for this day. I packed and left, ready to make it happen.

A few things were slightly wet when I packed up, and I planned to air them out later. My Milepost information was damp. That is the book that lists, mile by mile, what I can expect along every Canadian and Alaska road. I brought only the segments that I planned to ride, and some of that became useless when Officer Williams convinced me to change my route upon entering Canada. But from this point, I needed the book segments available for the Yukon and Alaska roads. I would make sure to dry them out before anything was damaged.

Some flat stretches and some minor climbing became quite scenic as I passed several lakes and the Rabid Grizzlies area. I didn't want to see a rabid one, but I did want to see a grizzly. My next conversation might have been intended to make me rethink that thought.

I met Juergen Schmidt, a veterinarian from Bavaria, Germany, who was cycling the Cassiar Highway much better prepared than I was. He'd had altercations already with two grizzlies, one of them in Fairbanks, and was now prepared with bear spray and a whistle. He considered getting an air horn too. We talked for a while about what was ahead for him, and he decided to take a rest day in Dease Lake. The nice people and the WiFi seemed to seal the deal.

Next came Jade City, as I passed the area where the mineral was mined and sold. There were no regular stores, but I was still in good shape. The wind was now a significant tailwind on a day that I needed it the most.

Only one more possible supply point existed until the end of the Cassiar, and the Milepost magazine said to call ahead because the store in Hope Lake was not always open. I pedaled on, mostly because my cell phone had no service and I had to go that way anyway. My water was getting low and I needed a few snacks for what would be a very long afternoon. I prayed that these things would be provided.

I found the store with about a dozen people standing outside it at a few minutes until 1 p.m. I heard them say the store would open today and that someone was on the way. In the meantime, one of the neighbors helped me get water out of a spigot at the back of the store. The water tasted bad and she let it run for a long time, improving the taste enough that I filled my bottles.

Once the store opened, a young Indian woman tried to help everyone. The inside of the store was about the size of a 12-by-12 room, and very limited items were scattered about. I bought several candy bars just to have a few more snacks.

The first miles north of Hope Lake were challenging; then they settled down as I climbed a bunch of small berms and coasted into flat riding between. Eventually, a new section of road, one of the best seen on the whole trip, was totally flat and straight for miles. Plus I still had the tailwind. Riding was great until it all changed.

The wind shifted at first to a side wind. The good pavement went away and some of the climbing became significant. Then came the final straw; a huge storm that I could see for miles ahead caught up. I had dressed for it and buttoned everything up, knowing that this one would be rough. I rode through a burned out forest as lightning crashed over and over nearby. Two girls stopped in a small pickup and one of them screamed, "There are trees being blown over just ahead!" I yelled back, "I don't have any place to go, except to keep riding." Well meaning, I am sure. I just didn't have any other options. Usually I can take these extremes pretty well, but the strikes were close, very close.

Along the way, I had seen some incredible mountains and nice lakes today. I was riding through an eerie forest that had been burned over, probably several years ago. What remained of the Cassiar Highway and B.C. 37 then became a very odd road. Some of the climbing was so steep that small vehicles must have trouble with it. I had to walk the worst of it, including one long, steep hill with no road shoulders and no guardrails. That left a drop-off of at least 100 feet in places. All of this was newly paved, and I later learned that this worst hill had its own webcam.

Off that monster, I rode up and down, up and down for more than 10 miles on steep but usually short hills that didn't fit the terrain. The hills had actually been manufactured. I was tired, close to the end of an incredible day of challenges, and all I was doing was riding this up and down craziness. Why had they made hills where none existed in this land of mountains and plentiful hills? I got the answer later.

Finally, I reached the end of the Cassiar Highway and entered the Yukon. I made a few photos, meagerly pumped a fist and left this world behind.

CHAPTER 7

The Yukon begins

Arriving in the Yukon was the goal for the day, that and finishing the Cassiar Highway. Late on this Sunday afternoon, I was very tired and ready to find a room. I had not called ahead; I simply couldn't get any cell coverage earlier and still didn't have it. Just ahead was the first settlement in the Yukon, the Northern Beaver Post and the Golden Nugget Truckstop. Shown on billboards as a one-stop remedy for just about anything needed, the truck stop had a gift shop, a café, motel and campground. I had turned on the Alaska Highway to continue north, ready to find a few comforts and end this very long day. Still, I was excited to begin my Yukon adventure, recalling times I had heard the name on old TV shows and movies.

I pedaled toward the front door of the café, the only building that had any activity. A much different experience than what I had expected began to develop. Seated in the café were about a dozen customers, all either eating or waiting on their food. At a few minutes before 9 p.m., I had no idea that the whole facility might be about to close, but that is what I was told. I needed food, a place to stay and WiFi. Very soon, I felt like a bother more than a customer.

I asked about a room and was told that there were none in the motel. According to the young guy at the cash register, I could either camp or get a sleeping room. Unsure what that was, I was told that the room had a bed and not much more. There would be shared showers and a bathroom, plus a TV room. When told that this room was $89 and he only had a couple rooms left, I asked about WiFi. The clerk said, "No, it's not included. WiFi is expensive out here." I told him about the newspaper, the fact that I needed to plan for the next few days and that I would be gone really early. Finally relenting on the WiFi after a call to the manager, he told me to walk over to the manager's office and I should be able to pick it up outside.

With one minor victory in my pocket and the grill about to close, I ordered two grilled cheese sandwiches and fries. The clerk had to ask the cook to confirm that I could get the food. They consented, and I began to gather up a few items. A decent display of pastries and pie slices was just in front of me, so I asked about them. The cinnamon buns and pie slices were $4.50 each. Next I asked about water. They said they couldn't give out water from the grill because of some Yukon ruling that I never understood. The café could only sell me bottles of water from a certain label, and they were $3.50 each. My bill for the room and the food came to $122. I asked about ice cream and was told that the café was closing. The clerk took time to charge my credit card and tell me vaguely where my room was.

I rolled the bike and the food around the complex and found the room and the shared bathroom area. The mosquitos were building as two guys worked hard to set up a tent, something I was glad not to do tonight. Unsure about this place, I had a late evening ahead with a story to write and, I hoped, some time and internet access to plan.

The complex was huge. Some parts of it were not open, such as the gift shop, and nothing at all seemed to be going on that looked like a truck stop. There was very little traffic late in the evening on the Alaska Highway. I saw other people, but none of them were friendly and I didn't have a single conversation. One attempt at asking for help in understanding the bathroom and shower system and where to find the manager's WiFi went nowhere. The TV room had an open door and, seeing feet, I walked in to ask questions. Mosquitos were flying and the guy was watching a documentary. I asked about the WiFi and he said, "Just take whatever you're using and walk back toward the café until the signal gets stronger. You'll know when you get there!" Enough said. Thank you very much!

I found the bathrooms but didn't take a shower because it was midnight by the time I finished the day's update and transmitted everything. I wanted to leave at no later than 6, making my per hour charge to sleep in the bed about $20 if

I could get there soon. But heck, I was in the Yukon!

The bike took up most of the foot space in the sleeping room. The bed was good, but then I think all beds are pretty much OK, especially after 110 miles. I slept quite well, leaving any effort at planning until the next morning.

I was amazed that five hours later, I had to venture north but couldn't find a single person to talk to before I left. I went back to the manager's office, looked up a few things, pulled out my Milepost section for the Alaska Highway and figured I would just have to wing it. Water looked to be very scarce. Just then, I saw the cook go in the back door to the café. He had not spoken to me the previous night but had remained busy. This was my chance to get some information on what to expect on the road ahead.

I introduced myself to Bob, the cook, and told him what I was doing. Suddenly I had found a friend. Bob was well versed on the two places ahead where I might get water and took time to tell me a little about where I might camp. There were no food stops ahead for the day, so I asked if he could sell me more pastries and water even if the café wasn't yet open. Bob agreed, and with a plastic bag full of $20 worth of needed supplies, I loaded my panniers and was yet again excited about the Alaska Highway. Past the one tractor-trailer at the "truck stop," I pedaled north toward more adventures.

Looking back on my night at the Nugget Truck Stop, I knew that it could have been much worse. And it might be for future cyclists. I noted a "For Sale" sign on the property as I left. The 110 miles I rode to get to a supply point at this truck stop might end up being 200 miles or more if the truck stop was forced to close.

A few miles up the road, with decent road shoulders to cycle on, I decided to stop and eat a snack. Seldom could I find anything along these remote roads to lean the bike against. I spotted a sign post that looked sturdy and had no trouble leaning the bike. Once done eating, I realized the dirt was very sandy. As I tried to push the bike back up on the road, it slipped sideways and both of us fell. It wasn't my first fall on the trip, but it was embarrassing to tumble while just pushing the bike. Not a big deal because no one else saw it happen.

The morning passed slowly with little scenery and plenty of up and down, though none was severe. I had the feeling that my effort was dragging after a long and steady climb finally finished off the morning. Shortly after, a much bigger event happened. I had finally topped the long climb and was making great time on the downside. Without any previous signs of bear scat or tracks that morning, I noticed a grizzly, my very first one of the trip, walking toward the road about 200 yards ahead. As the bear reached the road, a tractor-trailer barreled by, missing the grizzly by less than six feet. The bear seemed shaken but walked into the road just as I got near him. I stopped and took a photo. Just then noticing me, the bear changed direction and headed toward me at a slow walk. Not thinking that I should wait for him at that spot, I dropped the iPad into the handlebar bag and started to pedal away.

For what seemed like a minute possibly, I just pedaled. Not alarmed initially, I wasn't pedaling intensely. Suddenly a small pickup truck pulled up beside me with a dog barking on the passenger seat. The woman behind the wheel pointed backwards and mouthed, "Look!" The bear was loping toward me and was only feet behind. My legs were suddenly energized and I had nothing to do but pedal. A tractor-trailer coming toward me from ahead was braking sharply. I kept pedaling and didn't look back until probably a quarter mile had passed. The road around me was empty in all directions.

Not sure what had just happened, I could only imagine that the truck was slowing so quickly to get between me and the bear. Or that the woman and the dog did something similar in their truck. I had heard of that tactic being used several times already. Either way, I counted myself very fortunate to leave this situation behind, and I pedaled away. To the best of my knowledge, no horns, thuds or unusual noises happened.

I later heard of a cyclist who stopped and tried to reason with a bear in the same situation. His bear eventually walked away. Not the best negotiator on someone else's turf, I fear things would have not turned out well had I tried that.

At the moment, all this didn't seem to be a huge deal.

After I had time to ride and reflect, the danger quotient seemed a little bigger. There was a story to share for the rest of my life, for sure. I had wanted to see a grizzly and I had. The veterinarian from Bavaria had encountered two aggressive grizzlies. Later I checked Google for other similar occurrences. The summer timeframe was full of them. One friend suggested that all the smoke from the local fires had the grizzlies wound up. Regardless, the slice of blueberry pie in my pannier remained safe.

Meanwhile, my water supply was running low. I stopped at an overlook and saw an RV parked nearby. I had learned that RVs had large water supplies and asked Lee and Jeannie Kanter if they could spare some. What followed was one of the best conversations of the trip, focused on lots of traveling. They filled all my empty bottles plus gave me another one. I would be good for the rest of the day.

As soon as I parted with the Kanters, cyclists Thomas Lesperrier and Lise Faron of Paris, France, met me coming up the next hill. Just having crossed some of the road repair, they had the dust and rough pavement on their minds. I dreaded the thought of it, hoping that this segment would not be so dusty. We also talked about a restaurant ahead that was fairly new, and a motel alongside.

On the trip so far, I kept eating more and more pastries. They were available, provided energy and didn't take a lot of space or weigh much. At this point, I was just getting by, and some issues were developing. One of them was an infected foot. What I thought was merely severe blistering had become much worse. Without a motel room, I was limited in what I could do. Right now, Vaseline and a healing lotion of some kind were my options. Camping in the woods didn't allow me to even clean my feet, as I should. Six days without a shower was a long time.

After a long climb but with a favorable tailwind, I wanted to go at least 15 more miles. I would be camping in the woods again, but the owner of the small store, restaurant and motel had some information that I needed. He told me there was nothing ahead for a long time. To meet my goals to make it to Anchorage, I knew I couldn't stay at this motel. There would be road construction off and on all the way to Whitehorse, the only decent-sized town left until Anchorage. It was too early in the afternoon, and with the wind favorable, I needed to keep riding. I bought some water and considered ordering something out of the restaurant, but nobody was in it. The stop was just a gas-snack option, a restaurant and small motel in the middle of nowhere. Two super large muffins for $5 each went in my bags.

I pedaled on into the unknown, once again not sure or really concerned where I would spend the night. The storeowner told me of a pretty place next to a stream about 15 miles ahead. My plans were derailed briefly when my front tire suddenly went flat, only the second one of the trip. A front tire flat is much easier to fix, simply because the tire comes off and goes back on the bike easily. There was no chain to get just right, one of the bigger challenges of changing the tube in a back tire.

Fixing the front tire means that just a few spins of the axle holder start the process. When loose enough, the rim simply will drop from the tire fork. Unhooking the brake is usually needed to make the tire come off easily. I let any remaining air out of the tire and unscrew a holding nut that secures the tube in place on the rim. Two tire irons are used to work the rim loose from the tire, allowing the tube to come out. Once the tube is out, I don't try to find a hole in it. In all my travels, I have never patched a tube, although some cyclists do this regularly. The problem with patching, if you can find the hole, is that it must be sealed perfectly to hold air. Too many times, the same tube has to be repaired again. That is not a solution that I want to waste time on.

Skipping ahead, I run my fingers around inside the rim and try to find something sharp that may have caused the flat. If something is in the rim or tire that damaged the recent tube and is not removed, it could get the next tube too. Small pieces of steel belt from car or truck tires have most often been the culprits. However, most of the time, I don't find anything that caused the flat. If not, a new tube goes in, which is often easier when just slightly inflated. I only use a pump if no CO_2 cartridges are available. The CO_2 cartridge inflates the tube with a tool that attaches to the tube. Once the tube is in, the tire goes back on. I make sure that none of the tube can be seen and the tire is seated correctly.

The tube holding nut is tightened, then the tire inflated. My rule of thumb is to inflate it just to the point that the tire is hard between my fingers. I then remount the tire, making sure to put it back on in the same direction.

Once the tire is back on, I repack everything, including the tools and old tube and any trash into my bags and often can get back to riding right away.

On this repair, I missed that the tire didn't seat perfectly when totally inflated, and it rode with a hard spot. The solution was to let some air out, make sure the tire was right and then re-inflate it. This lengthy process took about 25 minutes, and during that time mosquitos bombarded me again. In certain areas, it was impossible to escape them. The best feeling was to finally start pushing those pedals and leave them behind. I hoped to still reach the suggested area to camp that night.

Pedaling hard and still making good time, I rode on and spotted a few likely camping spots too early. Every time I stopped the bike, the mosquitos came at me. This was going to be a tough camping night. The terrain was flat, the wind was gentle and lots of water was around. The mosquitos needed someone to munch on.

I found the place the store owner suggested, centered on a quickly moving stream. What surprised me was a no-trespassing sign and some paving equipment parked nearby. I decided to camp there anyway, with 86 miles complete. I knew those biting bastards were coming again. Usually that word was not in my vocabulary, but I was very much looking forward to a night inside a motel on the following night. My feet needed work, my body didn't deserve any more bites and I needed a good night's sleep.

Putting the tent up as quickly as possible in the edge of the woods was the drill again. I rushed and got it done, then pitched my stuff inside, remembering to button up the bags in case it should rain. One of the muffins went inside along with the sleeping bag, the air pad, my phone and iPad, one of my panniers with the soft stuff to use for a pillow, my long pants because it would get cold overnight and a few other odds and ends. I squashed all the mosquitos possible on my legs and dove in. Two big tent zippers were usually the final thing to do, but one was in sad shape and the panel next to it had started to tear away. I propped up the bad place on the tent and then finally started killing the mosquitos that made it in the tent. Once that was done, I could start to relax. Imagine doing this every night, then doing it in reverse only a few hours later!

One thing that happened in the tent was of note. I really didn't want to take my socks off because it would get cold later. However, my feet needed to air out, especially the foul smelling left one. I had begun to worry about the foot because just walking was painful enough that it reminded me of the issue with every step. I pulled the socks off and pitched them in the corner. Very soon, the tent smelled like the left foot.

Just as I did every morning in the tent, I awoke to see the mosquitos buzzing outside the screen and excited about when I would come out. For the first time, I dug out the Amazon mosquito net and put it on. With the long pants on too, I ventured out and vowed to do this every remaining day that I camped. A few mosquitos got inside the netting and they were frustrating, but my legs and the rest of my body were fairly well covered. I noticed them landing on odd things like the bike seat and probably trying to bite it. A friend later told me that I should have been tucking the corners of the net into my jacket or shirt.

Once packed up, I hit the Alaska Highway again. Road work was on again and off again, slowing my progress. A much longer than usual segment of roadway was being torn up, but this group had decided to water down the dust. I wondered why the rest didn't do the same thing. A large water truck, similar to a milk truck at home, was constantly driving back and forth, dropping a lane wide width of water on the road. I was so excited that I waved at the guy every time he came by. Breathing was easy on this day.

I headed for Teslin and a hoped-for motel for the evening. Teslin came not too long after another section of road that was being torn up. This time lots of state workers were on duty, helping to keep the pace lower on the vehicles as they passed through. I honestly can't describe how inconsiderate the truckers in this area had been. Maybe it's because they are paid by the load and try to make as many as possible. Nothing about the rocks and gravel bouncing off their trucks and trailers could be good as they barreled through the construction areas. The times that the drivers chose to get too close to me, maybe just for fun, were the worst. But at least on this segment they didn't get the chance. Lead cars kept them under control. I laughed when the trucks had to stop and then drive slow.

One long brutal climb and then a pleasant downhill brought me to the big bridge just before Teslin. I walked the bike across because of the hard metal grating and some small missing floor segments along the way. These were no problem for a car, but the bike tire could slip into one of the missing segments and either damage the bike or flip me off of it while riding.

I had been watching billboards to see the things offered in Teslin. Several motels, a truck stop and a restaurant were the first things I saw, plus a few houses. I actually rode through the whole town in two minutes, with my first stop at the truck stop and grocery. The truck stop had a motel too, and I inquired about a room. None were available but they pointed me toward a larger place across the street, complete with an attached campground and restaurant. I was overcome with the need to find a place soon, partly because of so much to do, but also because I needed to work on my feet.

I walked the bike over to the bigger motel and asked. No rooms were available here either; the clerk put me on the waiting list in case someone canceled. I noticed the restaurant and read the menu. I promised to be back for the reasonably priced veggie burger. Since my cell phone still had no signal, the clerk couldn't call, but I agreed to check back.

There was one motel left, more a part of a hunting and fishing lodge. The nice folks at the truck stop said these rooms were cheaper, all different and might not have WiFi. I walked the bike across the street and looked for someone to help me. A sign on the door said to call a cell number for assistance, which certainly would not work for me. So I began to look around. With a few buildings on site, I found no one around until a woman hollered from the second floor of the office. She had a room for the night and said the owner was around somewhere and would have more. Doug Martens soon popped out of one of the smaller buildings, saying he had been taking a nap.

Doug made his living as a hunting and fishing guide and mostly used his lodge to house customers before and after trips. I told him I needed a room and at present the other two places were full. Doug had rooms, he said, and then I asked about those in a larger and separate building. Doug said, "I use them when I need them, but the only open one is not in the best of shape. It was used for a residence for a while and we haven't fixed it back yet." Doug's price for a room was $80 a night and the other motels wanted $120. "But if you want to save some money, I will do this room for $40 cash," Doug said. We looked at the large room. It had all I needed but was definitely not prepared for regular tenants. I had a nice shower, a huge bed and sort of a kitchen. The WiFi was great. The room didn't have a chair, a TV or any weather control other than working windows, and all were open. I sealed the deal with cash and put the bike on the back porch, which became an issue later.

With a room in hand and some extra cash in my pocket, I walked back to the restaurant and got the veggie burger and a big brownie. No one had canceled a room, but I was set. I got a lawn chair from Doug and spread my stuff out for the day's update and a complete repacking of my bags. I envisioned a long hot shower and a better night's rest than any lately.

I had to deal with my sleep deficit very soon. Twice so far, I had almost fallen asleep on the bike, one time complete with hallucinations. Never before had this happened. I had been coasting down from a long climb and realized that my concentration was lacking. My eyes were extremely heavy and suddenly I sensed that my control was slipping. I dreamed of crashing the bike — all of this as part of a sort of dopey state. It was not pleasant at all. I stopped the bike, got off and tried to clear my head.

With all the holes in the road recently, I had to be alert at all times. A crash would be the disaster that I've yet to experience on one of these adventures. Promising myself to be in bed by 9 p.m., I went back to work.

Outside, rain had begun to fall steadily and with some

wind involved. I didn't have to worry for once. I was inside and all my things were dry. There would be no suffering from the cold or danger from lightning this time. I began to dream of a big day tomorrow, with some long miles possibly due to Doug's description of the upcoming terrain, a couple of food and water stops and the impending restful night.

Whitehorse was coming up soon. If I needed something, there wouldn't be a better place to get it. With about 25,000 residents, it equaled the population of the rest of the Yukon. Should I break down and buy the bear spray and the mosquito repellent, or even replace my falling-apart tent? The ride was nearing about 75%, Anchorage was just 10 or so days away. No doubt, this was my biggest challenge on the bike yet. Running out of water, low on food and surviving on Pop-Tarts, I was on a ride that topped all others on overall difficulty. The possible title for my next book had entered my mind, but there was plenty of riding time to think it through.

Not a single day had been easy. Unexpected challenges had become the norm. But I loved pedaling away from my overnight camping spot and noticing wet bear tracks in the road. As tough as this ride was, I wanted to experience it all!

Back to reality. As the rain fell outside, I finished my story, repacked my bags, took that first shower in six days, worked on my feet and got squared away for bed. I felt content and more at peace than I had for days.

During the night, there was a huge crash outside, probably on the porch. Close to 2 a.m., I was wide-awake and realized that the bike was still on that porch. Where would I be if the bike was gone? I got up, made sure the bike was OK and returned to bed. I had three more hours of glorious sleep remaining. No doubt, I was again asleep immediately.

Amazingly refreshed, and clean too, I began the new day's process at 5 a.m. My left foot felt better, even if it wasn't. My goal early was to cover as much as 115 miles, but factors could certainly affect that total. I packed the bike and rolled it out to the road. I was ready to mount up when I realized that the front tire was a tad down on air. I chose to air it back up quickly and see what happened as I rode north.

What followed was one of the most pleasant early morning rides to date. As I rode out of Teslin, nothing was open, not even the truck stop. Surprised by this, I was confident that enough supplies were packed to make the next supply point. The Teslin Lake was on my left for 32 miles, nearly all of that scenic and with moderate terrain. An occasional vehicle passed by, but for the most part I had this early morning to myself.

Later in the morning, I made Johnson's Crossing at the Teslin River Bridge after 45 miles of riding. Pleased enough with that total, and definitely interested in this historic place, I stopped to sample the café's trademark pastries. Johnson's Crossing had been a significant supply point during construction of the Alaska Highway. Right then, it was significant to me because I was hungry. Inside I found Jane

Clyde and a wonderful array of food and pastry choices. She took my order for an egg and cheese sandwich while I took a little longer to decide how much space my bags had for the famous cinnamon buns. They were huge and priced right, especially on the day-old rack. I made a sizable purchase and was excited enough to take a few extra minutes to eat. The egg and cheese biscuit was huge and so were the cinnamon buns. Before I left, one of each had been deposited into my stomach, thus requiring no bag space.

I took a few minutes to look around. With a small motel and campground, Johnson's Crossing would have been a nice place to spend a couple of days. It had views of the river and scenic mountains, as well as an onsite campground and motel. Gas and diesel were also available at this wonderful place. Although the stop took too long, I thoroughly enjoyed it.

Back on the road, I had to ride upwards away from the river. This was often the punishment for the downhill on the other side, but OK in the vast scheme of things. In a moment of revelation and amazement, I happened to look at my phone and saw that I had a bar just as I topped the highest point. A complication to the rest of my journey had earlier developed, and I needed to get a phone call or two out for help.

When working on the infected left foot, I noticed that my feet and ankles were swollen on both sides. Very aware that the swelling was a strong symptom of the blood clots that have followed several of my earlier rides, I decided to email my doctor's assistant, and see what they thought. I was afraid to disregard the swelling and knew that if I needed to start on blood thinner, getting it was going to be a challenge.

I got the message out and that started a chain of events that would eventually bring some blood thinner to me with daughter Amber's arrival in Anchorage. I was not worried that I had a serious clot yet, because my breathing was good and my strength was excellent, both of which would have been issues. From this call, Christy Harrison tried to arrange a pickup at a pharmacy in Whitehorse, but due to Canadian law, prescriptions from the U.S. were not allowed. She suggested a stop by the E.R. in Whitehorse, something that Amber advocated too. I knew from the start that I wouldn't do it. Getting the medicine when I saw Amber in Anchorage would be fine, and then the blood thinner would be in place for the long flights home, another issue.

Just as I pedaled off the top of that hill, I wondered if there would be more points of connection later that day. Almost immediately, I saw Bill Brooks of Sidney, British Columbia, pedaling toward me. He was in a rush, evidently a little behind his planned cycling schedule toward Vancouver. I got a quick photo, he did too, and then Bill was gone.

Not long afterward, I enjoyed a new experience for my cycling adventures. Yusuke Yamamaka of Japan came toward me, and we both were happy to stop and talk. Yusuke was on a long journey to Argentina and had what looked like the best and newest equipment. Four bags full and a little more tied on made a good load for his bike. We had just begun to talk about his journey and equipment when suddenly Tom De Wilde of Belgium pedaled up. Tom was also going to Argentina, and that seemed to shock both of the young riders. They were on the same road, going to the same place, and had not seen each other until this point. Tom had minimal equipment, probably the least I had ever seen on a genuine long-distance cyclist. His tent, small and light, was attached the front fork of the bike. One other bag was all he had. Had I seen Tom on the road and not talked with him, I would have waved him off as someone who was riding in a group or had a vehicle following with his gear. Honestly, and I will only say it for the first time in this book, those who carry their own gear and deal with the daily issues think of themselves differently. Just a slightly higher risk taker and adventurer might be enough said, because no one else would come along later to solve your issues. Tom and Yusuke were bonding as we shared "Safe travels" and I rode on north.

The real trial of the day was just beginning. A windy period had started, and the lingering smoke in the area was stronger too. As I got farther down the road, I reacquired my cell signal on occasion, and Siri told me about a motel ahead that Milepost didn't seem to know about. It was half the distance to Whitehorse and reachable if I pushed it. I clicked on the link without really looking at the town, and Siri assured me that the motel was just 13 miles away. The terrain had become very hilly all of a sudden, and the wind was a hindrance too. Nobody answered at the motel and I hoped it was still open and had rooms available. The only way to find out was to get them to answer the call.

I rode and called when I had the signal, and with no answer, rode some more. I was on the right road and getting closer, according to Siri. Down to then 9 miles, then 5, and I still couldn't get an answer. I texted my technical advisor Amanda Lewis back home, and she went to work on getting the motel on the phone. Meanwhile, I rode into the wind and up and down hills, slowly getting closer per Siri. Amanda secured a room and I kept riding on past where the motel should have been. There were signs for a couple of bed and breakfast places, but the motel never came in sight. All the while, Siri said I was just a mile away but never any closer.

I asked a local resident who was turning into a driveway to help me. He looked at my screen and said that Siri missed this one. He thought the motel was on this road but way ahead in Haine's Junction. Turns out he was right. The resident said that just ahead was one of the best campgrounds in the area, the Caribou RV Park, part of the Good Sam system.

I rode into the RV park and found the office closed, but the manager was close by. Just in time, I got the code for the showers and bathroom and headed to find a campsite. Right away, I saw this was in fact a good campground and had fewer mosquitos. I can't begin to say how pleasant that was. All my newspaper stuff was taken care of at the adjacent picnic table and transmitted at near midnight, followed by a quick shower and a short night's sleep.

Nine days of riding remained, and Milepost said 735 miles — still significant but doable.

CHAPTER 8

Whitehorse and on to Beaver Creek

Clean again, I had celebrated with a shower on the second straight day. I got to work briefly on my infected foot and expected a little more improvement. Additionally, I had something similar to a tennis elbow developing. Both of these were firsts. I also missed a morning of mosquito bites. All this happened at the Caribou RV Park. Whitehorse was just ahead.

On my mind was the front tire going slack. I began to wonder if I should stop at a bike shop and get it looked at while in Whitehorse, but surely nothing much would be open on July 4. I usually looked for a rodeo on my previous rides and actually had found one in the Badlands. Nobody mentioned a rodeo or any celebration here. I wondered why.

Then, as I rode toward Whitehorse, I noticed lots of traffic inbound. The road was slow and hilly too, with plenty of cars zooming past, very odd for a holiday. I really stuck my foot in it when a cyclist on the way to work stopped and asked if I needed anything. I asked Amos, "Do you know of any bike shops that might be open today?" He replied, "Probably all of them; it's just a regular workday." Suddenly my mind woke up to the fact that I was in Canada, where they certainly wouldn't celebrate the Fourth of July. I guess I really was tired.

The bike shop took first priority, next to stopping at McDonald's for Egg McMuffins. I got them, caught up on some messages, ordered a few pastries and went to find the bike shop. One shop was particularly big and not far away, and I honestly didn't explore the others. Amos had the idea of fixing the bike by going to places other than a bike shop, which didn't seem right to me. He mentioned a very big and busy place called Canadian Tire, much like a Walmart, with an emphasis on mechanical things. I stopped by and quickly figured that the fit was not right.

During this time of Whitehorse discovery, I asked a woman in a SUV for directions by waving at her and asking her to roll the window down. She happily responded and off we rode in separate directions. That became significant later.

A much different kind of guy on a bike had been checking for cigarette butts in a designated smoking area ahead. When I asked if he knew of the specific bike shop, he said, "Sure follow me!" I hated that idea, but I did it. We rode to the first bike shop he had in mind, and it was closed. We went to the second, probably 10 blocks away and also not the one I had looked up. This was a nice shop called Cadence Cycle. Seeing customers, lots of inventory and bustling activity, I didn't expect immediate service. The butt guy on the bike asked me to give him some money "for chips," which I declined. He had taken me to the wrong bike shop and took way longer to find another. Later, I wished I had given him a small amount of money.

Cadence Cycle was first-class, and Abel asked, "How can I help?" I told him about my trip and that I was unsure of why the front tire continued to leak slowly. To my surprise, Abel jumped right on it and rolled the bike to a portable work stand. We took the panniers off and he mounted the bike on the work stand, took the front tire off and proceeded to remove the tire and tube. Taking special care with the rim, he squirted something, possibly water, on the inside of the rim. Feeling slowly for any imperfections, Abel didn't find any reason for the leak. We decided to insert a brand new tube, thinking the first one may have been defective. To my amazement and with deft precision, Abel inserted the tube and mounted the tire without using any tools. I couldn't have done it this way, but with a skilled technician doing the work I felt confident that the air leak was a thing of the past.

Abel was from France and had been in Canada for only 10 months. Very personable and talented, he clearly enjoyed his work and the conversation as well. I bought CO_2 cartridges, enough to surely finish my trip. I am sure Abel charged me for parts only and no labor, adding to a wonderful experience. My stops at bike shops across the U.S. and Canada almost always go well, and I think it adds a little excitement to their day to hear about my solo cycling adventures.

Abel told me where to find the S.S. Klondike, a historic ore hauling paddle wheeler that was the centerpiece of an interesting downtown. With the tire and rim checked out so quickly, I decided to explore the downtown before venturing back north. The old city area had plenty of restored buildings and a walking/running/cycling path that was like a busy river walk. The old depot stood out as significant too, making me wish I could take longer to explore. The busy streets in this area belied the 25,000 residents, as many as in all the rest of the Yukon province put together.

Knowing I needed to make lots of miles, I finally headed north and tried to remember what Abel said was the best way out of town. I knew a significant climb was in front of me. The descent to the river level of the downtown had been an easy coast. Now payback was coming.

Just before leaving, I wanted to make sure I had food and water for the rest of the day and who knows what later. Another McDonald's stop started an interesting sequence of events. I ordered more pastries and another Egg McMuffin. Three times, the card machine wouldn't accept my credit card. I had begun to pull out my debit card to use when I got an email on my phone about fraudulent card activity. I responded that the charges in Whitehorse were legitimate and almost immediately the first card was accepted. Bank of America was on the watch — a good thing.

Intent on changing out of cold weather morning clothes, I went into the bathroom. I heard a conversation just outside the door between two guys, one of whom said, "See my bike over there; it's all loaded and ready to go!" and he laughed big. I came out and just for fun asked him, "So how is the best way out town on a bicycle?" He deadpanned, "I don't know, I don't have a bike." I laughed on the way out the door. The wise guy of course had been talking about my bike.

Two more small instances also occurred, both of which surprised me. I had asked for a water cup. Some McDonald's will only give out a super small cup for free and others don't care. In this store, I was given a medium cup and stood at the ice and water tab just a little long, according to one customer who said, "So, are you about through?" I told him I was sorry and moved over to the side, thinking the conversation was over. The man filled his cup and said, "So, are we OK?" I just walked away as I replied, "Sure."

Another guy, with two women in tow, seemed perturbed that he had to walk around my bike on the sidewalk. With plenty of room to spare, he scowled at me. Saying something to one of the women, he opened the door and turned to scowl at me again. I smiled and rolled the bike away, ready to leave this town.

With only 25 miles complete and the morning almost

gone, I had to get going. The big and harsh uphill did come and was so bad that I stopped to eat at the top of it, getting a plan together as Whitehorse would soon be behind me.

Aware that the last store for miles was coming up, I stopped to get a little more food and enjoyed a conversation with the not-too-busy clerk. He told me I would find good places to camp going north and would love the rest areas, since the Yukon took pride in both of these things. The clerk also told me I could drink any of the free-flowing water ahead. Except, he said, "if it has been used by beavers; you don't want 'beaver fever!'" I decided to try to avoid the free-flowing water as long as I could.

Back on the road, those headed for the Klondike soon turned off, and the Alaska Highway became low-traffic again. The riding became less challenging and much prettier. I had either good shoulders or the car lane to myself, leaving no traffic issues at all.

A familiar car came toward me and pulled off the road. It was Deb Jutra, the same woman I had asked for directions earlier that day. Deb said there was a store much nearer than I thought. Based on her projections, I could make it that evening, at least before dark. Dark was coming about 11 p.m. during this Yukon segment, so I had plenty of time. She turned around and went back the way she came, and it was suddenly apparent that this trip was just to help me. Deb then headed for a social event and concert of some kind.

Still later, on her way back to Whitehorse, Deb found me again. Her event was over, and she stopped again to make sure I was OK. No other vehicles were on the road at that time, and I was making great time by riding in the car lane. One car or truck every 20 minutes came by and I could always hear them coming from a long way back. Snow-covered mountains were off to the left front and were spectacular. The serious miles were starting to add up and I had reachable goals, albeit with a still long evening ahead. No matter, riding like this at a good pace with nice scenery was close to the ultimate for me.

If anything, the traffic lessened as twilight began to set in. Storm clouds were ahead too and looked serious. A grizzly, this time calm and focused on what he was eating, barely gave me a glance from 50 feet away. Reluctant now to wild camp in the area, I decided to continue on to the store and adjacent campground that Deb had mentioned. Occasional lightning lit the clouds far ahead and made the evening even more eventful, especially once the rain finally started.

I found the store, which appeared to be part of a truck stop and was closed. No trucks were there but a few people were camping, notably a couple of motorcycle riders. They were sleeping under a tarp they had put up. I cringed at the thought of how many mosquitos might be feeding on them.

The rain came hard enough that setting up the tent let portions of it get wet. The mosquitos hit me even in the rain, so I had double the reason to hustle. With just enough of the tent up and not staked down, I dove in at nearly midnight. I had exceeded the mileage portion of the day's goal by completing 96 miles. My legs seemed to have wings all afternoon — a wonderful feeling.

My cell phone still didn't work and Siri was of little use. I asked her for some directional help and all I got was, "I don't know where you are!"

The road surfaces kept changing and I always needed to be on the lookout for potholes. On some of the better pavement, the bike appeared to speed up and riding was much easier. Changing road surfaces were likely to continue as Alaska was just ahead.

I do like camping in the rain quite a bit, but only if the rain doesn't start until after the tent is up. The worst of last night's rain fell when I started to put it up. As a result, lots of my things were damp. The tent had begun to show even more wear, and it never seemed to get totally dry with all the early morning packing and late evening unpacking. I can't remember such ongoing dampness as an issue before, especially on mostly dry days.

I left the campground very early in search of more of that fast road. Gradually the road became more challenging, but the scenery got better and better. The Kluane Mountain Range ice fields were amazingly beautiful as I headed toward them. Mt. Kennedy and Mt. Hubbard were two of the best known and tallest of that range.

More campgrounds were along the way, with some private and some free. The government ones were free but had very few amenities. I pedaled into Haines Junction, heading downhill for a while but with huge snowcapped mountains in front of me. Haines Junction seemed to be full of small motels, restaurants and convenience stores. I stopped at what I think was the nicest store twice, and actually stayed for some time. I bought a good supply of food and ate part of it while writing my recap of yesterday's events. Some WiFi and cell connectivity was available, and I knew it wouldn't be for much longer. I was headed into more wilderness. Three Indian women told me I was about 200 miles from the Alaska border.

After leaving the store once, I came back to buy more food. Based on what I knew of the road ahead, the Alaska Highway was about to get remote again. The clerk in the store told me to expect some hard climbing and then it would even out. That climbing began just a short ride down the road, but still in sight of those beautiful mountains, now much closer. Just as I started to climb, two SUV loads of women pulled over to visit and offer food. Hikers Bev, Paula, Patti, Sherri, Sharon, Angie and Shirley were lots of fun and offered to take me for a meal after. I couldn't take time to do that but certainly enjoyed seeing all of them.

Then came the long and steady climb. On and on for 4-5-mph slogs and getting warmer as I went, the top couldn't have come soon enough. The scenery had gone away and the area looked much more like a high desert with scrub trees and bushes. Just for fun, the Alaska Highway's second and third highest peaks came virtually back to back. As the temperature rose, the wind did too. Once I topped the first peak, I began to think this would be a miserable afternoon. As I topped that peak, I saw a Japanese cyclist coming toward me. I waited and tried to talk with him, but he was virtually incoherent and maybe couldn't understand English. Mostly he offered grunts and stares. I talked with a cyclist later who also met him, and all she got was the same thing. I hope he made it, and in his favor was a strong tailwind.

The worst afternoon of the trip began. The wind was pushing back at me and at least some climbing continued — not as severe but steady, which contributed to greater than expected water consumption. I had my head down, pedaling forward, and saw only two cyclists briefly in the other lane. They were taking advantage of a tailwind and were obviously aware that I was suffering. On I rode, just happy for every mile I could make.

One woman stopped to see if I was OK. I probably looked worse than I was but continued to ride with my head down. I asked if she had water, and she didn't. She offered to take me to the nearest stream. "We drink from it all the time. The water is good," she said. Knowing the stream was just 4-5 miles ahead, I assured her I would make that.

Something better than drinking out of the stream happened next. On a good downhill, I happened to see Bryan Troll walking his dog near his RV. I pulled over, told Bryan what I was doing and asked if he might be able to spare some water. "Of course, but I don't have any good containers," he said. I told him I had plenty of containers and would be set for the evening if he just filled them. Bryan did that and we had a good talk afterwards. He had bought a small RV from a relative and was taking his niece to see a bunch of national parks and other attractions up the west coast over the summer. She was headed back to school soon. Once that happened, Bryan planned to keep going. They were going to Alaska that night and had just stopped for a short while. Luckily, I happened by at just the right time.

Bryan, from Philadelphia, was possibly the best conversation of the whole trip. For once, I was not in a hurry and my pace was so slow, I envisioned this being the evening when I might have to ride all night. Bryan's niece joined the conversation briefly, which I took as a signal they needed to get rolling. So did I, with one of the last big climbs right in front of me.

As I started that climb, I sent an email to a friend who had a circle of available prayer warriors. I asked if we could all have prayer together and ask for the travel to get easier soon. It seemed selfish at the time and I wondered whether to do it. Her response came right back and the prayers started.

I climbed the big hill, stopped for a snack now that I had plenty of water, and did my part of the prayer. Already, on the other side of the big hill, the wind seemed less. What happened next astounded me. We had prayed to help me get out of this hot, dry, very hilly experience and that I would make better time as the day headed toward evening. Within 20 minutes I started a miraculous downhill that stretched out for 20 miles. Spectacular scenery soon filled in all around me. The wind didn't totally die down, but it sure got better.

I knew of a campground ahead and pedaled that way. With occasional gusts now that I was riding along the Kluane Lake, the sand and dirt battered me, but another quick turn reduced the wind. Being off the high ridge and mountains probably were the biggest factors. Occasionally the hills and mountains seemed to shield the wind. Then, just as quickly, they briefly funneled it.

Milepost had told me about the campground, on the lake, and I figured that the breezes would keep the mosquitos somewhat at bay. "No camping" signs had been posted along the section of road where the lake view was the best. With making consistent miles on my mind, I couldn't have stopped in this area anyway.

At the entrance to the campground were posted "No Vacancy" signs. That was a disappointment, as was the long and steep downhill to the campground itself. If I rode down and was refused, I had a big and mean climb to get back to where I was. Just at the same time, Joe Troyer and his SUV with trailer pulled in and also saw the signs. Joe and his family were returning to their home in Alaska. I knew of a nearby free campground too and after a good conversation, Joe headed that way.

With 73 miles done on this super-challenging day, I found a nearby spot in the woods and set up camp. Hidden from the road, but still in one of those no camping places, I set up the tent and went right to work to prepare my story for the day. I kept nodding off and simply could not stay awake to put my thoughts together. For the first time on this trip, I gave up and went right to sleep. My sleep deficit was becoming worse daily.

Remembering the trial of the previous day's wind, I got up a little extra early in hopes of grabbing some time on the road while the breezes remained calm. My mind was on getting to see Destruction Bay, another place that is often mentioned on TV, especially the Ice Road Truckers. There seemed a certain mystique for the area and I imagined Destruction Bay as a special place.

About 12 miles into the morning ride, I found a very nice convenience store, café and motel that formed most of Destruction Bay. Inside the store, I found some things I wanted to add to my bags and asked about egg, cheese and tomato biscuits at the restaurant. Those were in my hands within minutes. The three workers I talked to were extremely nice, maintaining smiles throughout our conversations. I noticed the store and probably the whole complex had WiFi. I asked the clerk if I could use it, to which he replied, "Sure, but don't do anything to tie it up. It isn't the best WiFi." While I ate the first biscuit, I went outside and transmitted pictures and a leftover update quite quickly. I went back and thanked the clerk and told him about the fast WiFi. I also noticed a surprisingly strong signal for Verizon too.

Destruction Bay got its name when a huge storm destroyed most of the buildings. The settlement began as a 100-mile relay station for truckers, equipped with rest and repair facilities. I noticed a few trucks and gas and fuel pumps that were fairly active.

A small group of cyclists had evidently camped on the property overnight and were getting ready to ride that day. One of them hollered from about 50-60 yards away and motioned me over. I kept going and figured I would see them later if they were headed north. There was no more time to kill while the wind was reasonably calm.

North of Destruction Bay, the terrain became very sparse and increasingly hilly. The pace was so slow that I envisioned losing some earlier gains on mileage toward Anchorage. The highlight of the morning came when the Troyer family stopped by. I expected not to see them anymore after they headed off to the free campground last night. Joe pulled over as I neared the top of a long grade and we talked about their issues with the campground, one that I had read about. Campers sleeping in tents or on the ground were supposed to sleep inside an electric fence. Joe's family didn't do it and got admonished by someone in authority for not following the rules. The Troyer family loaded me up with grapes and other snacks. Those grapes were the best thing I ate all day.

Next came a little community called Burwash Landing. The clerk at Haines Junction and the woman who wanted me to drink from the river both said Burwash Landing would have a store and that it was the next available supply point after Haines Junction. Both must have forgotten about the nice facilities at Destruction Bay. And as it turned out, there was no store at Burwash Landing.

Oddly, as I rode through the area, an SUV slowed and a woman waved at me from the passenger side window. The vehicle kept hitting the brakes as if they planned to stop, but then rode on not to be seen again. On a whim, I checked the radio and found a strong station, which was unusual for such a remote area. The station quickly faded and was gone within three miles.

Two cyclists pedaled toward me, just after motorists started flashing their lights. I met Pierre and Alexandria, another couple from Paris, France, and asked if there were bears or anything unusual ahead. They hadn't seen anything, so we talked about the road both north and south. The couple hoped to make Destruction Bay and I assured them that they could. I found out about a campground ahead that just might fit. Their main question was if I had enjoyed the Cassiar Highway because they were considering not using it. I told them of my experiences with the bears and supply points, plus the scenery and the challenging riding. I didn't want to strongly steer them either way, but realized they were still considering going the longer and somewhat easier route around it. We waved goodbye and I felt stronger now knowing the road ahead would be less hilly for a while. I envisioned a better afternoon and hoped to go for a big day.

The smoke in the air was building and the afternoon breezes were blowing it toward me. I didn't think much of it until a woman pulled over to my lane in the road. "You're going to have to turn around and go back. You can't get through," she said. "The fire is coming this way and all traffic is stopped ahead at the rest area." I had no idea how to do what she suggested, so I questioned her more. She said, "The fire people have closed the road and say it won't be open until tomorrow. I don't know what to do either. I am going to my house and let my kids know what's happening. They will be worried that they haven't heard from me. My cell phone only works in a small area just ahead." The woman assured me I could get to the rest area, but no farther. She estimated the rest area was 20 miles ahead.

I thanked her and rode on. As usual, there was very little traffic and the cars I did meet had no interest in me. The smoke in the air thickened as I continued to ride. Milepost reported that a government campground just ahead had a water source. With the unsure fire situation ahead, I decided to stop and top off my bottles. This was all a new experience for me. With food in my bags and enough water, I felt better about my options, especially if there was some delay.

Inside the large campground, I couldn't find a water source. I asked a few campers and was no better off until a couple from Kentucky told me the water pump had been removed. They proceeded to give me several bottles of water and topped off my other bottles too. We shared our experiences and a few laughs over Canadians making fun of our Southern drawls.

I rode away from the campground with pleasant memories of that couple and resolved to figure out the fire situation. Best I could tell, there were no other routes available and I sure was not going to turn back. I kept riding north toward the fire. The sky now looked cloudy from the smoke, but I had no problems breathing.

As I rode into the evening, already with enough to worry about, another long segment of torn-up road appeared. This one had lots of loose gravel. Some of the gravel was so thick that I sought portions of the road with some of the solid base still intact. I kept riding back and forth over both lanes in hopes of keeping the bike upright while making at least a decent pace. At one point, about a dozen cars and trucks came toward me at a high rate of speed, raising more of that choking dust and slinging rocks. Then they were gone. The Alaska Highway sure continued to be a challenge.

A few minutes later, a single car pulled to my side and stopped. The family inside wanted me to know the road was still blocked and that I could stay at the rest area. I asked if I could get to a campground that was ahead. The couple in the front seat both replied that I could. "You are almost there. It's just ahead. We saw lots of tents," the woman said. It had been a long day and the riding was still slow on the loose gravel, so just ahead would be fine with me.

After 96 miles of riding, my Saturday evening was spent at Discovery Yukon Lodgings, a high-end campground. The office was closed as I rode into the facility and saw a group sitting and laughing at a picnic table. I asked if the campground was still taking campers and one guy seemed to step forward. "Just go find an open place and you can see where the others have set up tents or are in their vehicles. Over there is the best place," he said. I asked about a bathroom or shower code, and he said there was none. I asked about WiFi and another person said, "It doesn't work; you're in the wilderness now." That seemed a smart aleck answer at the end of a long day, so I just said, "Well, I have just ridden here from Nevada and I've seen wilderness much worse than this." Suddenly, the conversation was less important, and I went to find a camp site. I saw a few glam camping setups, my first ever. Glam camping is where a nice room, complete with a bed and furniture, is set up inside a heavy zip-up tarp. It's similar to moving a bedroom out to a campground; I guess you can still call it camping. Those campsites had cars parked outside.

I sat down and caught up my update, ending about midnight yet again, and then put up my tent. I got started the next morning after a decent sleep of four and a half hours, ready to go find out if I could get through the fire. The folks at the picnic table the night before had differing opinions on when it would be possible to get through.

Packed and ready to go, I tried to find somebody official to pay. No one was in the office, nobody was moving around, and I couldn't wait. There was no drop box that I could find either, so I decided to send back a check once I arrived home. I rode on to find a way through the fire.

Having never experienced a nearby forest fire in my cycling travels, I had no idea what to expect on this morning. An adventure within itself was possible as I pedaled toward the smoke, wondering what I could do if not allowed to pass. About 20 minutes was the interval between oncoming vehicles and nobody seemed to be hurrying or with an urgent purpose.

I passed the rest stop and saw people camping there too, but not nearly as many vehicles as I expected. Still, I bet the bathrooms got a workout last evening. The lack of vehicles made me hope that the road was open ahead and only the late sleepers remained.

Just past the rest stop was a fire fighter waiting beside a pickup with an orange flag. She waved me to a stop and said, "We are letting people through for now, and as you can see, not a whole lot is actively burning. Just keep moving and watch for fire vehicles."

I did as she said and was astounded. For at least five miles on both sides of the road, and as far as I could see off in the distance, the fire was still smoking. Some hot spots were actively burning. I could see where a large lake had stopped its progress in one area. It was an eerie ride, with all the fire's devastating power evident as I rode along. The smoke was fairly heavy but didn't bother me as I rode. If anything, I was excited to see this up close and I took a few photos. The last official fire personnel presence was the pickup on the other end of the worst devastation. He just waved me through and then got back inside the running pickup.

Just ahead was Beaver Creek, the last town in the Yukon before crossing into Alaska. According to Milepost, Beaver Creek had almost anything that I needed, but my first priority was a stop at the visitor center. I envisioned getting some information on what was ahead, charging my iPad and phone, maybe even charging the solar battery packs before stopping to load my bags with food and water. Finishing and submitting my update and photos would help too.

The visitor center was on my left upon entering the town. Liane was on duty and helped me tremendously. I told her about my trip and that I needed to charge things and complete my updates before sending to the Post. She was agreeable to all that and told me that I could set up on the front porch where an outdoor receptacle was available. I told her of my idea to cross the border ahead and ride on a significant distance to Northway Junction where I thought I could get supplies and camp. Liane confirmed that I could, in fact, do this, and said the ride was long and challenging.

But I remembered many times later that day when she confirmed food and camping available in Northway Junction.

With my electronic things charging as fast as possible, I set aside an hour to catch up on messages and updates while using the visitor center WiFi. My items sufficiently charged, I went back in and thanked Liane. I helped her find the Post updates on her computer and asked which of the stores would have the best quantities of snacks for my ride ahead. She suggested the one with a polar bear statue out front, and I headed that way with a final thank you.

I won't mention the name of the polar bear store because I entered what seemed an overpriced tourist trap. Items of interest were as much as three times what I expected to pay. Small brownies, 2 inches square and fresh baked, were $3.50 each. One sleeve of Pop Tarts was $3 — not a box, but one sleeve sold individually. I bought a few snacks and some high-priced water because I had to have it, and decided to take a chance that I could find better deals in Northway Junction that evening. For once, I left one of these stores still hungry. After all, my emergency Pop-Tarts were still available and waiting in my bag.

Just ahead was Alaska. I was ready. My infected foot was still not sufficiently addressed, and the smoke was a constant. What else would the Alaska Highway have for me?

CHAPTER 9

Finally, Alaska!

After the odd reception from one of the customs officers when I entered Canada from Oroville, Washington, I didn't know what to expect as I was about to enter Alaska. In a way, Alaska had been on my mind for the last six years as the push to cycle through all 50 states continued. The 49th entry into the United States of America, Alaska was also about to be my 49th state. I thought back over my history of cycling the nation and wondered if anyone had ever cycled through in each state's order of entry into the country. With mine this close to completion, I will pass that idea and opportunity on to others.

I rode on from Beaver Creek, the Yukon, and found some ultra-challenging hills on a super smoky morning. Some of the hills were picturesque too. Near the top of one was the "Welcome to Alaska" sign. Expecting this sign once I passed through customs and not before, I pulled the bike over and got set up for the most important photo of the whole trip. Two people were checking out the area, and I got one of them to snap the photos that defined the trip. I was in Alaska, evidently, but still had to pass through customs.

Once done with the celebratory photos, I rode on up the hill to find a long line of RVs and other vehicles waiting. I was unsure what to do and waited briefly behind the last in line RV. Seeing no movement, I remembered what happened a few years back when I entered Canada near Buffalo. Another cyclist told me that we got priority. "Just ride to the front of the line," he said. And he was right. The line was very long, with multiple lanes full. I rode to the front and waited until the next car got entry. Then an agent called me over. That Canadian agent was extremely nice, much like Officer Williams during my recent Canadian customs entrance.

Entering into the U.S. was new for me. I hoped for the best. I even opened my panniers just in case they wanted to look in them; the process would be easier. I walked the bike to the front of the line and the driver of the lead car motioned me on. That was cool, but I watched for the customs agent to agree and he did. Two agents were working the line. The male of the pair took my passport and right away asked, "Did you see the fires?" I told him that I did see the one near Beaver Creek. By that time, he had processed me and said, "Enjoy Alaska!" That was all it took.

The first part of the Alaska Highway that was actually in Alaska began as freshly paved and beautiful. After a flat start, the road began to climb steadily. The quality of the road wasn't as nice later, and eventually it became as bad as I had seen. With big hills and poor roads, I didn't like the first part of Alaska so far. The scenery didn't excite me either.

My sole focus was to find the Northway Truck Stop and complete another long day. More up and down kept coming, all the while dodging holes in the road. There was little traffic, and the afternoon began to slide away. Once, with what the sign said was 10 miles to go, I finally saw Northway mentioned. The Northway Junction was where I would spend the night. Liane at the Beaver Creek visitor center confirmed it would be a good place for food and camping.

Those last 10 miles from the sign took 14, meaning that the distance was off on the sign and that total agreed with the distance sheet Liane had provided. My bike cyclometer confirmed Liane's distance. Past tired for a day that began long ago on the other side of the fires, I finally found the place I was looking for. And I found the biggest disappointment I could remember!

There was a store with gas pumps and what used to be a campground. At just past 8 p.m., not a single person was around. Two vehicles that looked unused for a while sat there, but I soon realized this was a part-time store now that specialized in crafts. I could see some snacks inside, but there was no real truck stop. The electrical plugs for the campground were disconnected. There were no bathrooms or showers.

Simply put, the place was a bust! And I was 50 miles

away from the next supply point. My water was gone, and I had little more than my emergency Pop-Tarts in my bags for food. I was disappointed and quickly went to work on trying to find water, my most pressing need. I could survive the night for sure on the Pop-Tarts. My mind was awhirl with possibilities. I read in Milepost that Northway also had an airport where small plane customs were done, and the community appeared to be spread thinly between the former truck stop and the airport, a distance of about four miles.

My one stroke of luck was that the Fish and Game complex was just down that road toward the airport. I walked the bike over there and found an office building, three cabins and what looked like a former community gathering place in an old barn-style building. I saw one guy driving out and flagged him down. I told him I needed water and that I was stuck without it. Clearly an employee of the Alaska Fish and Game Department, he first told me he didn't know anything about water there. I told him, "A building this size has to have water and, if you work here, you know where it is. I just rode here from the other side of Beaver Creek and this store is supposed to be open and camping available here, according to the visitor center there."

He started off with a useless reply: "This is Alaska; people around here are headed home by this time." He began walking and pointed at the side of the office building to two spigots. "One of those is hot, the other is cold, I don't know which. Don't tell anybody I told you where they are," he said. I immediately thought, "Wouldn't you want people to know that you helped?" But I didn't say it because he was already in his truck, driving away.

I filled my bottles and was set for water for the night. At the time, I considered riding on to the next town. Light would be in the sky for at least three more hours, and I put batteries in my flashing red light on the back of the bike. I could do that, or I could sit at a picnic table and do my story for the day and sleep in my tent, right where the old campground used to be. An early start would be easy with nothing here to keep me.

After a few minutes of thought, I decided to do my writing and get what sleep I could right there. I hoped somebody would stop by to complain. A long day with 94 miles complete was my reward. Pop-Tarts and water tasted just fine as I weighed progress made.

The night passed with a few interruptions. With lots of daylight until way late, people kept coming by the store and what appeared to be the neighborhood dumpster. Once when I looked out while this was going on, the folks dropping off trash waved at me. The mosquitos were present but not terrible, and the failing tent kept most of them out. Truck and car noise on the Alaska Highway were nearly non-existent.

I was ready early to roll toward Tok, my next destination. The experience of Northway Junction was one that I could put behind me. I planned to email Liane at the Beaver Creek Visitor Center and let her know the situation with the camping and store. Otherwise, there was no need in looking backwards. Just five days of riding remained.

This was going to be a short day, leaving time to do a few things and get some needed rest. By taking the afternoon off, I could rest, work on my feet, wash my clothes, heal up a little bit and plan for the final push toward Anchorage. At this point, just the thought of a shower was motivating enough to get the bike on the road a few minutes earlier than planned.

The ride to Tok was unremarkable, challenging in the beginning but much better later. I met Brett Woodward of Chesapeake, Virginia. I had seen few Americans who were on long rides. Brett and a friend were riding to New Mexico just in time to experience the hot Southwest temperatures. Brett told me about part of the Glenn Highway ahead and the remaining portion of the Alaska Highway. I couldn't help him much because his route was going to be significantly different from mine.

Brett mentioned a major road repair ahead, much more involved than the others I had passed. He and his friend were made to put their bikes on a pilot truck to pass through the area. I didn't think much of it at the time but would later.

Wondering why Americans don't do the long bicycle rides as much as those from other countries was on my mind. All the cyclists from other countries that I have met were excited about being in the United States, and Canada too. They call the United States beautiful whenever I ask about why they came.

The last 10 miles into Tok were flat, and a portion of it passed through construction. The weather was beautiful. I thought briefly of continuing on, and riding for more miles at the expense of the creature comforts already mentioned. But the afternoon off was the best thing to do and I definitely needed it. Just 49 miles complete left me to average 82 during the last four days on the road.

Tok and the Three Bears Motel were both wonderful. I had spent so much time sleeping in the woods and riding in the wilderness that this small town and modest motel seemed like New York City and the Waldorf Astoria to me. I was surrounded by everything I could possibly want. I came to the Three Bears Motel after being referred by the first place I called. There were plenty of choices, but the Three Bears had a small mini-mart inside the lobby. I would later learn that Three Bears was a significant company that also owned the grocery and a separate convenience store that coupled with a huge hunting/fishing/camping store.

I was hungry when I hit town and the very first stop was the convenience store. I was shocked to find "back home North Carolina prices" on snacks, drinks and even gasoline. A steady stream of happy customers came through as I realized I wanted some of everything. The pleasant clerks appeared happy to be working and smiled all the way through their efficient portion of the operation. I vowed to eat up and return.

My visit to the grocery store was even more phenomenal. Choices everywhere, with normal prices — even bananas at 44 cents a pound, just like at home. Big donuts and cookies were a dollar. I saw yogurts of all kinds and plenty of pre-made sandwiches. I just couldn't imagine such a place. Was this the best town ever!

The town of Tok began in 1942 with the construction of the Alaska Highway. So much material was handled through the area that it was called the "Million Dollar Camp." The town faced destruction in 1990, when lightning sparked a fire that more than 1,000 firefighters couldn't stop. A miracle wind arose just as the fire neared the first building and blew the fire away. Tok — meaning "peaceful crossing," according to one source — has a population of more than 1,200 people.

Back in the room, I was ready to eat, catch up my writing and do all the other things already mentioned. I started with attention to my feet, following a shower. The shower felt so good, lingering in the hot water in the middle of the afternoon. I wore the towel around for a while, especially after washing out all my running clothes. On the whole trip, I never stopped once for a laundromat or used a motel washer and dryer. I didn't see either one more than a handful of times, and whenever I could take a shower, I included washing out my base layer most times. The shorts did the whole trip, the cycling shirt did most of it and I rotated three pairs of socks — especially with the gruesome smell of that left foot.

My first look at myself in a mirror was a shock. My upper body was extremely thin and my abs were the tightest ever, with veins popping and ribs showing. My face and neck were very thin. My eyes were tired. All of this was the result of the significant challenge of cycling the north country.

I was learning through frustration about connectivity on this trip. Once I was ready to make my reports and send photos, I could get the motel's WiFi. However, the strength of signal was terrible. Using my iPad, I didn't have enough signal strength to download messages and certainly could not have sent photos out. I asked one of the motel employees why the signal was so poor, and he said this was a constant all over town. The employee reset the system twice in hopes it would improve. It did not.

I noticed my AT&T signal was a solid four bars, an uncommon occurrence for any time during this trip. I relaxed and knew that I could use the phone for a hotspot to allow the iPad work to be transmitted. After setting the hotspot up that afternoon, I may have had the best connectivity in town. All my information was sent easily, and I was able to plan for the next few days. The motel manager later told me AT&T had recently installed a new tower nearby.

With plans to get done early with everything, including a complete repack of my bags and another trip to the grocery store, I wanted to be in bed by 8 p.m. I made it at 9, by far the earliest of the trip. The sleep was deep and peaceful, and I woke up in time to load the bike before the motel breakfast building opened. Yes, the Three Bears Motel had a separate building just for us to get a wonderful continental breakfast. Issued with each key was a pass code to the breakfast building. In all my travels, I had never seen this. The breakfast had lots of great choices, some of which made it to my bags.

I rode out of the motel lot and turned onto the Glenn Highway for the first time. For all its good and bad, I said goodbye to the Alaska Highway, the single most challenging road I have ever ridden for such length. Still in a valley of sorts, the first 10 miles were flat, and I had a strong gospel station to enjoy on the radio.

A moose walked close to the road and then back into the woods just as a camper pickup came by. About that same time, I realized that I still had the room key in my pocket. Now five miles away, I couldn't go back and resolved to mail the key back to the motel. I planned to enjoy the ride and listen to the radio from North Pole, Alaska. A favorite pastime on this trip, listening to the radio gave me insight into the people and issues facing the local communities. It was very odd that this station had 50,000 watts and such coverage. Other stations were small and lasted only a few miles. Easily 90% of the time, a radio signal was not available.

The air was full of smoke, making the sky look cloudy or

foggy. The radio announcer talked about fires in the area still not under control. The smoke had become so low-hanging that I could not see the many mountaintops in the area. More mountains were just ahead, reportedly some of the best of the trip. No significant rain was in the forecast, and the wind had settled to a modest breeze. I may miss the tops of those upcoming mountains too.

I met Roman Durren of Oberegg, Switzerland, as he pedaled north. It seemed odd at the time, but my direction was now to the southwest after all the riding north. Roman was a carefree guy, not worried about making a certain distance each day. I told him about Tok and how nice the people were, and within minutes he decided to stay the night there. While many of the Post's readers had chastised me for spending so many nights sleeping in the woods, Roman took it to another level by sleeping under a bridge last night. Roman was probably going to Vancouver but was unsure. We had a nice talk and eventually rode our separate ways. Just five minutes after he had gone, I remembered the motel room key and realized that Roman would have been glad to drop it off at Three Bears.

Having been told road conditions were going to improve nearer Anchorage, I soon entered the one segment of the trip that still bothers me. I noticed several "Road Construction Ahead" signs, each becoming more elaborate as I pedaled on. With not a lot of traffic, I didn't think there would be much of a delay or any real issues.

I found where the traffic was stopped and rode right up to the flagman, as I always do. Right away, the flagman and another guy started telling me that I would have to have the bike shuttled across this construction. I immediately disagreed. I told them how far I was riding and that, in all of my previous trips, never had my bike been put inside or onto another vehicle. The flagman told me that I could be arrested in Alaska if I refused their direction and proceeded to tell me about another case where he was called to court to testify about what had happened.

Other motorists began to listen while the flagman called his supervisor, who happened to be driving a pilot truck. The construction was being done over a 10-mile segment of the road and much of the pavement was gone. She said, "We will stop you if you try to ride and state troopers will be called." I told her they could not stop me and said how important the whole length of the ride was to me. One of the motorists said, "Why are you taking so much time with this guy? We need to get through too."

I felt bad about what was occurring, but I also didn't want to have the bike hauled through the work area. Countless times, I had ridden through areas similar to this. I didn't know anything about this Alaska law, and of course my phone wouldn't work to have any chance to research it. The supervisor relented enough to say that I could ride through the area if I waited until construction was completed for the day, about two hours later.

There was a lot to process here, and I waited while the next group of motorists was taken through. I was nearly out of water again and the flagman, who seemed genuinely concerned, got me a fresh bottle. I didn't want to wait two more hours and I had made Alaska already, the ultimate goal of the trip. I noticed a pickup driver listening in on the conversation who seemed interested. Weighing everything and the fact that tonight had nothing assured, I asked the driver if we could put my bike in his truck for the ride across. "Sure," he said, "and I have a peanut butter and jelly sandwich for you too, and some Gatorade." So, we loaded the bike and I told the flagman.

My mood was ruined but the decision seemed the only right one in this case. I was all but out of supplies and had originally wanted another 100-mile day. It was impossible to get it if I stayed here waiting, and I had no time to get arrested if that was a real threat. There was only one store in that 100 miles and it wouldn't stay open late; none of them do in the remote parts of Canada that I had passed. I had to make that store for supplies. I resigned myself to ride in the back of the truck with my bike.

That ride was at 35 to 40 mph across about 8-10 miles of the construction. Significant yes, but not worse than I had seen in other areas. The road was sprayed wet, and I ended up with a dirty coating of gravel water on the bike and me. All the cars and trucks were dirty messes after the crossing. We unloaded the bike and my bags and I got my bearings on what needed to be done.

I had wasted miles and time on this mess and knew I had to hustle to find Posty's Store, the only supply point for 150 miles from Tok to Glennallen. Milepost told me I would arrive at about 7 p.m. if all went well and the terrain didn't get worse. I pedaled for all I was worth, hoping the store would still be open.

I found Posty's and saw the flagman already there. Bernie was his name and we talked briefly in a friendly way. He told me that the store closed in 10 minutes and proceeded to try to get some air into his truck tire. The store had just enough of a selection that I could get what I needed. The owner and her clerk were both friendly too and told me to take my time because they wouldn't actually close until 7:30 p.m. I made one supply run and went back for a little more, knowing that I had to ride at least half the day tomorrow before another store would be available.

We also talked about the Red Eagle Lodge just ahead. The owner knew a little about the lodge and said they had no food supplies but would probably provide breakfast. She said prices were reasonable if they had any space, so I decided to check out the place that was now just down the road about two miles. It was at least 30 more miles to any alternative lodging that was in fact a similar type place. Today had been the warmest day of the journey so far, with one customer at the store saying the high had been 91 degrees nearby. I also had noticed the days shortening slightly, at 4-6 minutes a day.

After what I counted later as my most frustrating experience of the trip, I found a bright spot. The Red Eagle Lodge was just what I needed. It included a collection of 100-year-old restored settlers' cabins of various sizes and a historic landing field for nearby bush pilots. I found a relaxing environment with a lot to offer. The owner or manager, I'm not sure which she was, found me a cabin for $80 a night with breakfast included the next morning. It was the smallest empty cabin she had left and I found it to be wonderful. With a ceiling fan and a screen window, plus a big bed, I was set. For those who visited in the winter, there was an antique potbelly stove. All the cabins were different, and most were filled on this night. "Experience real Alaska of the 1920s" was the theme.

Usually breakfast at the Red Eagle Lodge was served starting about 7 a.m., but when I told her that I had to be on the road by 6 a.m., I got special consideration. I never take time to sit down for a breakfast meal because it's the best time to make time on the roads, with the least traffic and wind. Gone by 7 a.m., I was thankful to leave with a good breakfast and a few things for my bags. The last 227 miles to Anchorage beckoned me.

With the smoke still a factor, the higher mountain tops remained obscured. The ride to Glennallen totaled 45 miles and went very well. I stopped at the visitor center and asked about the road ahead and if any motels fit my projected mileage for the day. I got great information and called ahead with my now working phone to the Nelchina Lodge. Pete answered and promised he would save a room for me. Based on how fast the morning ride went, I expected about a 5 p.m. arrival and told Pete so.

The Glenn Highway began a steady 12-mile climb and even had one place with signage directed toward viewing specific nearby scenic mountains. I couldn't see a thing due to smoke. Still, the day's ride to this point had been wonderful, and I was looking forward to an early afternoon off the bike seat. All day, I had a moderate tailwind until a storm developed ahead of me. Serious-looking clouds hung on the southern horizon, and the consequence was a dramatic change in the winds. Within minutes, I was pummeled by an estimated 30 mph wind directly into my face. Pedaling forward was no longer easy and my pace slowed considerably. I hoped this would be temporary and that the storm would pass soon.

Although I never felt more than a drizzle, the south wind significantly changed the rest of the day. Instead of an early arrival over what was just moderately challenging terrain, I struggled to make any decent pace. The minutes and hours faded away as I continued on. Without service again, I couldn't call and verify my room at the motel.

I stopped at the small grocery that Pete told me about and bought some things for the evening and the next morning. An unusual grocery, it also had a towing service, and no one else was there except the owner. In fact, when I entered the store, which had things piled around in no real order, no one seemed to be there. Once I had about six items in my arms, including a couple of frozen egg and cheese biscuits, the owner came into the store. He totaled the items using a calculator and told me that the motel was still at least 10 miles away. I envisioned two more hours of riding and a near-dark arrival, wondering if I would still have a room.

Back on the damp road and into the breeze again, I got a pleasant surprise. I had seen the same motorcycle pass me numerous times as I rode north, the rider distinguished by his long hair and loaded bike. The last few times he passed, we had waved to each other. Juan Jerez passed me again, just as I left the grocery. This time, Juan pulled over and waited on me. I was happy to meet him and excited about the story of Juan's own journey.

Juan started a year of traveling in San Jose, California, and began working his way toward Alaska. My first sighting of Juan was in British Columbia and we had followed the same route since. Juan had camping lined up nearby and I had a motel, so this might not be our last sighting. The two of us shared a certain kindred spirit, and I could have easily spent hours talking with Juan. He was an adventurer for sure, headed for Costa Rica.

As we parted, my ride still had miles to go. If anything, the terrain worsened. Finally, after a long afternoon and 91 miles for the day, I rode into the parking lot of Nelchina

Lodge. Pete, the owner, was talking with a woman nearby and noticed me. He came over and said with a smile, "You did make it, I knew you would, even with the big storm!" Pete had saved my room even though he had a full house after my arrival. I learned that the storm had been strong in this area, with both wind and heavy rain. Pete was interesting in many ways, a sort of health and fitness nut who told me that his kids were all born at home and had never been to a doctor. All remained extremely healthy and never sick. If not for the pressing need to complete my reports, we probably could have talked for hours.

Pete offered me a frozen pizza and gave me some aloe to drink. He also showed me his basement workout room, surprisingly not heated in the cold months. My room was perfect for rolling the bike into or leaving it on the balcony outside, and Pete stopped by to make sure everything was in order. Pete used to live in Minnesota and grew up in Duluth, one of my favorite places on the northern tour bike ride.

I wrote and ate, had another wonderful shower while washing clothes, and hit the bed on time. On time meant before 11 p.m. these days, but I couldn't be happier. Two days of riding remained and my plans after an Anchorage arrival were coming together. My feet were getting better but most likely would heal faster after getting off the bike.

The owner of the grocery store told me the next day's riding would be as bad as I had seen, some of it with no room for the bike. Not sure exactly what he meant, I asked Pete about this. Pete agreed that some of it would be challenging but didn't expect such a terrible day. Pete even told me about a stop ahead to get either gravy biscuits, not really my thing, or something else.

The wind was already blowing, more of a side wind thankfully. By now, near the end of the trip, I came to realize that the wind blows just about every day in Canada and Alaska. I was not far from the Pacific Ocean and the Inland Passage that the cruise ships take. That explained some of the recurring west winds, and the weather fronts probably had something to do with the north winds. I couldn't recall many days that the wind was consistent from any direction for a whole day. It usually blew the strongest after 3 p.m., settling often but not always after 7 or 8 p.m.

Another long climb over the Glacier View peak led to the stop that Pete had earlier mentioned at the Eureka Lodge and Restaurant. I asked about an egg and cheese sandwich and was given a price of $13. I passed on that initially and ordered some cookies and a huge cinnamon bun from the pastry shelf. After some contemplation, I asked again about the sandwich and was informed the waitress had given me the wrong price. The correct price was $9. The explanation was that she thought I wanted bacon. Still too high but I took it. This would be my last food stop, according to the staff, on a long day that would be complete with plenty of challenges.

The smoke still obscured a lot of the scenery. Many of

the distant mountains were hazy this morning. Especially interesting to me was the Metanuska Glacier, seen for miles along the Glenn Highway. We couldn't get very close, but plenty of pull-offs for viewing were available. The glacier stretched 27 miles and the runoff started a huge river. The glacier near its terminus was four miles wide at one point and had remained fairly stable for 400 years.

While viewing the glacier, Juan Jerez passed me for the last time on his motorcycle, complete with his signature wave of the hand and big smile. I said a prayer later that he remains safe on his long journey.

I noticed there were in fact places to eat, at least one that offered pizza for glacier viewing. Other services connected to the glacier were helicopter flights and ATV rides to the site.

Past the glacier, the road width and safety issues became a concern. This must have been the portion of the road that the grocery owner had in mind. The road became narrow and curvy, many of them blind. Initially, I was so concerned that I walked the bike on the opposite side of the road for a mile or more in heavier-than-usual traffic. Realizing I had to take a chance on my safety to make the distance, I got back on the bike and rode up and down and around the curves. The edge of the road ended in a rock wall a few times, leaving zero chance to get off the road. It was so tight that I watched RV motorhomes meet a few times with not enough room to get past until I cleared. This was the single scariest section of the road on the Alaska adventure.

Finally past all this, with a few rain showers falling, I got a text from Janis Ramsey that she and her husband, Frank, still wanted to see me on the ride toward Anchorage if possible. Janis had been following my ride from the beginning and had contacted me early about stopping by. Frank was born and raised in Salisbury and was a football star for Boyden High School, the earlier name for Salisbury High. I had cleared the bad area with the tight curves and was within normal riding distance to Anchorage for the next day by that time. I looked forward to meeting Frank and Janis.

After several texts back and forth, Janis sent Frank to pick me up and we met near mile marker 71. Frank and I loaded the bike and all the bags on his truck, introduced ourselves, and then headed back to their home between Palmer and Wasilla, Alaska. Frank had left Salisbury after high school and became an Air Force pilot during the Vietnam War. After his service, Frank married Janis from Iowa and they moved to Alaska. Frank had a plane in the beginning and later sold it, although he continued his avocation as a professional hunting guide.

The ride back to their home was very pleasant while Janis was preparing a vegetarian dinner for all of us. Once settled into my room at their beautiful home, we all sat down to that dinner. The dining room looked over a beautiful lake, and easy conversation flowed for quite a while. In the back of my mind was the need to get my reports in so that I could easily move on to the last riding day into Anchorage. The subject matter was so interesting that I just couldn't pull away until after I was stuffed on Janis' rhubarb cake. We made plans to meet again in October in Salisbury when Frank and Janis would return for Frank's high school reunion.

By the time I gave up the conversation and went back to my room, I was so tired that I couldn't keep my eyes open to write, and a shower was out of the question. This day's 73 miles had just about done me in, particularly the mentally challenging segment on the narrow roads. Another deep sleep was just ahead. Frank and I planned to return the bike and me to mile marker 71 and the beginning of the final day's journey. Anchorage was just ahead.

CHAPTER 10

On to Anchorage and more, finally home

Frank Ramsey was up and ready to go early, waiting for me to drag my bags upstairs. As always, I enjoyed the hours of sleep that I got and, just as common, awoke excited for the day ahead. We loaded the bike into the bed of Frank's truck and headed north again, back to mile marker 71. On the ride out, which took a little over 30 minutes, I saw the terrain that I would return southwest on. These directions still seemed odd after so many miles of heading north on the bike. Only one hill was significant and there would be some scenery. The road shoulder looked good for the most part, and the weather was likely to be good. Low-hanging clouds looked threatening, but the forecast called for little chance of anything more than light rain.

We struggled a little bit to find the exact unloading point but found the driveway after we passed it by earlier. After a quick unload, Frank held the bike while I mounted the bags on the frame. We shook hands, I said my "Lord, ride with me today" daily prayer and it was back to work. Anchorage lay ahead.

Though the weather was not cold by Anchorage standards, I was chilly. I had on three shirts and my mittens to start, expecting to take some of it off later. I expected a good day, not particularly challenging. My big goal for the day was to press on into Anchorage and find the visitor center in search of more information about what would happen once the riding part of this adventure was done. Originally, I had a bigger plan but readjusted once I realized what was involved. Alaska and Canada are huge and not quite as easily connected as had I thought before beginning this adventure.

Less than 20 miles into the day's ride, I pedaled into Sutton. The town had a bar, a general store, a fire department and some nice people. For consistency's sake, I stopped at the general store for a short break and to pick up a few snacks. The clerk in the store had a distinct Southern drawl, maybe worse than mine. I asked her how she came to Alaska. Originally from Kentucky, she wouldn't say much about why she got to Sutton but told me how much she loved living there. I asked about the cold and dark winters and she steered the focus toward the good people who were especially welcoming. I sensed some issues with her past, especially after she said, "I've got a good husband now and we have built a nice life here." I got a good deal on a couple of huge blueberry muffins, just a dollar apiece and well under the going rate, along with plenty of laughter before I left.

On the way out to the bike, a local resident came over and wanted to know where I was riding. When I said, "Anchorage!" he seemed deflated. Then I added, "After more than 3,000 miles!" We talked for a few minutes, again with this guy telling me about how great living in Alaska was. Frank Ramsey had mentioned to me that there are no local police in this area and that state troopers address serious issues, often from hundreds of miles away. Frank also said that sometimes the local residents settle things themselves, as you might imagine, not in the best way.

Back on the road, I rode on to Palmer, a more modern town with lots of amenities. Serious paving work was going on, and not just the resurfacing that I had seen so much. This paving was reworking intersections and even some side roads. My goal was to stop at McDonald's and take a few minutes to use the WiFi. My previous day's update needed work, and I wanted to find the location and best route to the Anchorage visitor center.

All these things happened, and I felt especially relaxed about the rest of the upcoming ride. Close to Palmer, the ride was nearly flat, and much of it was on new and smooth pavement. I had ridden on so much of the rocky repaving that this smooth asphalt certainly took much less effort. Construction equipment was moving about, and I passed one place with a flag girl holding up traffic intermittently. With a smile, she waved me on through with, "Just stay on the right shoulder." That was the correct way to do it, much better than the disaster just a couple of days before. About 40 miles remained, all of which I hoped to enjoy.

I had been reminded that the home stretch to Anchorage was not flat. Within the last 30 miles, traffic was by far the heaviest that I had seen on the trip. The good shoulder remained and the road had improved, but traffic volume and speed meant no more riding in the road. There were a few long grades as the miles wound down, with not much scenery. I passed the Air Force base on the right, complete with a running and cycling path that followed the highway. A few cyclists were using it, but nobody else appeared to be ending a long ride.

Anchorage has about 300,000 residents, and many of them were driving that day. Once I made the downtown area, which was not large, I stopped at a car dealership where a salesman was watching me ride by. He told me the visitor center was just down Fourth Street and then over to Fifth. Anchorage didn't leave much room for bikes in the downtown, but with a few honks, I got there.

Without any fanfare for my arrival, I pulled over and celebrated at the official "Anchorage Welcomes You" sign. This ride had been my hardest to date and it had more challenges than any other. Lots more on that later!

The short ride to the visitor center put me right in the middle of the downtown area. The small visitor center was staffed by at least three women. Most people seemed to be just looking around and leaving, but I needed lots of specific information. One of the women was not busy when I leaned the bike against a corner of the building and walked in. I needed to find out if I could ride the train to meet the Alaska Ferry on its way south. I wanted to know the ferry's schedule and if I had time to catch up to it on the way south toward Bellingham, Washington.

My immediate need was to find a room for the night, hoping for something affordable. Within minutes, I found out that downtown Anchorage motels and hotels were very expensive. Two of the women in the visitor center were now listening to me, but apparently my questions were unusual. I told them that I had traveled by bicycle from Nevada and needed an economical room for one night and possibly two. One of them handed me a listing of local lodging, most of which were upper-end places. They circled a few and I went outside to call them. Most had nothing open, but one woman told me about her last available room. "I have this one room with no microwave or refrigerator and the shower is tight, a standup style. You can have it for $187, a 10% discount," she said. I passed, but later wondered about the shower description.

I called the local hostel and got an offer of $99 for a bunk and room where I could put my bike. My next call was to Christina Grande, a friend of cyclist Mary Rosser back home. Christina works at The Bike Shop in Anchorage, from which I would eventually ship the bike home. Christina suggested Airbnb and emailed me a couple of places.

One of those worked out, about four miles away and priced at $61 for the night. I got to see more of Anchorage and actually rode past The Bike Shop.

I settled in for the night with a wonderful host, and my reporting was easy. I still had only basic information about the Alaska Ferry and where I might go to find more details about the train. Regardless, I had the more immediate need to work out meeting my daughter and her husband the next morning at the airport after their cruise. I also had to pick up a rental car and drop off the bike for shipping home. The major work of the ride to Alaska and Anchorage was in the bag. Now some other cleanup details for that adventure and planning for the next week of activity were on tap as I began to entertain thoughts of returning home.

I found out from Amber that a bus from the cruise ship would arrive at the airport about 9:30 a.m. Saturday. I was just another six-mile ride from the airport Avis, where we already had the car rented. I left the Airbnb early the next morning and listened to Siri as she helped me find Avis. While waiting on the cruise bus, I dumped out my pannier cycling bags and repacked them, one for shipping home with the bike and another for remaining with me.

Amber and Jamie arrived, and we got a car for them and headed for The Bike Shop. My arrival on the bike was a few minutes after theirs, but we quickly dropped off the bike for shipment home. It was a major turning of the page as the bike was no longer my form of transportation and we saw it rolled away.

The bike, my Surly Long Haul Trucker, had earned its name with almost perfect operation for the 3,174 total miles of the cycling adventure. I will have more about the bike specifically later, but it had once again served its purpose as a dependable friend and workhorse. No mechanical issues, and only two flat tires, was way better than I could have expected at the outset back in Carson City, Nevada. The flats beat my longtime average of one per thousand miles ridden, almost unheard of among cyclists.

Back to downtown Anchorage. We found the visitor center again, and Amber and Jamie decided where they wanted to go. At the suggestion of a very sharp woman there, we decided to take the next two days and visit the Kenai Peninsula and Seward. More fires were threatening other areas and these places looked good for uninterrupted travel. Seward was about two hours away, and the drive was all along the coast and the railroad line that provided new ocean and inland passage views. Amber and Jamie had a flight back to North Carolina late on Sunday evening, so we soon headed out to make the best of what was left of their two days in Alaska. They had already sampled reindeer meat. My travel plans were still up in the air.

We drove southwest on the Seward Highway and followed another recommendation to stop at the Alaska Wildlife Center. This was a sprawling complex with lots of habitat pens for native animals that were being rehabilitated. Parking was jammed, with tour groups and other tourists wanting to see the native animals up close. The day was chilly and breezy while we walked around to see bears, reindeer, caribou, elk, foxes and others. At one point I was four feet from a bald eagle.

Farther on, we stopped at Seward, founded in 1898 as part of a trail system used by miners to drop off gold and pick up supplies. Seward grew quickly, and soon dog team mushers were delivering loads to Nome and later to other points. Mile 0, or the beginning of these famous trails, became the original starting point of the Iditarod sled dog race that continues today. The starting point is no longer in Seward but now follows other designated routes. The original trail is still open for exercise and history enthusiasts to cover by foot, bicycle or vehicle.

After looking around in Seward, we struggled to find an affordable place there for the night. We found a great deal at Cooper Landing on the Kenai River, at a place called the Grizzly Ridge Lodge. We got the upstairs of the very nice lodge with an amazing amount of room, wonderful views and friendly owners. A convenience store was across the road, and several motels and restaurants were close by.

Gold was discovered here in 1884 near the outlet of Kenai Lake into the Kenai River. The beautiful green river flowed by across the road from the lodge and behind the convenience store. It was easy to be relaxed while here, and I needed that. This was another place worth spending a few days, but we had to be back in Anchorage for the next phase of our trips.

We ate breakfast at a local restaurant on Sunday morning. The servings were huge and so was the bill. Interesting was the waitress, who moved to Alaska from Georgia for a change in her life. She has a small son and talked about having one of the only year-round fulltime jobs in their community. The waitress said there was so much to do nearby even in the long and dark winter, while I wondered if I could stand such a winter.

By noon, we headed back toward Anchorage and again enjoyed the beautiful roadway. We stopped by Girdwood, drove to Mt. Alyeska and found a nice waterfall, all part of the Chugach Mountains. Girdwood has been called "Glacier City," and we got good photos of one glacier from a winding dirt road towards a trailhead for Mt. Alyeska.

We rode back to Anchorage and walked around the downtown area again, stopping to eat. Along the way, we proceeded to lose where the car was parked. It was worth it to walk and stretch out my legs. Once we found the car, they wanted to head for the airport and not rush through security. I searched for another Airbnb for the night, didn't do as well and called a motel near the airport that I had seen on the bike ride the previous day.

I won't name the motel but will describe the experience. As with every other motel I called, this one's price seemed quite high. So I rolled the dice and said, "I just got here yesterday on my bicycle after riding from Nevada. I'm flying out in the morning if all goes well, and just need a place for the night. I will be leaving early." The owner of the motel backtracked on his price and cut it in half. I had a room for $60 and was asked a lot of questions about the bike ride, conditions, how long and more. It was fun to talk with the guy on the phone and I looked forward to meeting him.

The motel looked sketchy from the outside but that didn't bother me. I had seen this many times before and then found a great room. Plus the owner told me that I would get his best room. He came from behind his counter and gave me a big hug and said, "You will like this room!"

I walked down the sidewalk, opened the door and saw the biggest motel room I had ever entered. The huge den-like room had kitchen-type things including a range and big refrigerator. There was a sink and some cabinets too. On toward the back were the bathroom and a huge bedroom area. Nothing wrong with any of this, but the room looked as though it was used for storage. It had lots of odd pieces in it. In addition to huge file cabinets and other furniture odds and ends, it had one of those huge TVs from years ago that you had to sit right in front of to see the picture. Even then, this one was barely visible.

The room was very clean and still had plenty of room to move around. It was cold in the room and the thermostat didn't work, but I found a small space heater and plugged it in until the seating area was comfortable. The WiFi password never worked, but both carriers had good signals so submitting my information was easy.

The night went well, complete with what was one of the best hot showers I had experienced, and the same for the bed. All in all, I saved money and smiled as I left early the next morning for the airport. I didn't see the owner again but promised him a book and will send it when complete.

I had pieced together a plan with the help of Janis Ramsey. I needed to get to Juneau to catch up with the Alaska Ferry. The train wouldn't get it done, so I had to take a flight from Anchorage on Alaska Air. With no rush to get to Juneau, I chose the middle of the day flight arrival, leaving plenty of time for security after returning the car to Avis. All that went well, as did my flight to Juneau.

Arrival at the Juneau airport, about six miles from town, started the next adventure. Once on the ground at the small airport, I asked for directions to town. Two locals told me, "Oh, you aren't going to walk it, are you? It is a long way, probably six miles, way too far to walk. Take the bus, it picks up right outside." I followed those instructions, waited 45 minutes on the next bus and paid $2 for a roundabout ride to the downtown Juneau Transportation Center. I found the Transportation Center to be a glassed-in structure where bus travelers could wait out of the weather. It was near the center of town. I asked the driver how to get to the ferry terminal and he said, "You can't get all the way there on the bus, but we can get you close." The ferry would board early the next morning at 2:45 a.m. I had a long wait, about 12 hours, but plenty to explore in the meantime. After 45 days of needing to be right on time for either running or cycling, with many miles to go, I was fine with the unchallenging time ahead. Just another extended adventure.

When I got off the bus, I asked another driver where I should catch the bus that would take me closest to the ferry. "Meet me right here at 11:30 p.m.," he said. "I'm the driver." That sounded good, and I headed out to the explore the town. Four or five cruise ships were docked in downtown Juneau. The sidewalks were jammed with people intent on doing touristy things. Some were riding a gondola to the top of a mountain, others were booking tours, and the rest were visiting the local shops. All this made me tired just watching it happen, so I found a good place and enjoyed watching people. A drizzly rain started, the first of four successive cloudy and rainy days.

I wandered around and stopped in a few shops and the drug store. Nothing much interested me, and the prices were very high. I read all the historical markers and walked up and down the streets to see the oldest buildings. By late afternoon, I spotted a Subway shop that had normal prices and was a little off the beaten path of the cruise ship folks. I picked up some food there, enjoyed an unhurried meal and watched in awe as one guy kept the store running by himself. I asked to charge my iPad and phone and he was happy to let me do it. A successive group of regulars came in to get their sandwiches. The easy camaraderie between the Subway guy and the customers was fun to watch.

I wandered around again and explored another part of town. The University of Alaska Southeast had a small campus in Juneau. Lots of students were standing around using their WiFi, so I tried as well. This one was password protected and I didn't really need it anyway. On I walked and began to wonder where the locals bought their goods. Surely they didn't pay the touristy prices that I saw downtown. I found directions to a Foodland online and walked about three more blocks that way, as the rain continued.

What I found was my savior for the rest of the long afternoon and long evening. The Foodland store was huge and had an Ace Hardware attached. I figured I needed to carry some snacks onto the ferry and was hungry enough to eat before then. With some room in my bag, I got enough to feel better should I need to eat again later. I knew little about the Alaska Ferry, but having food already in my possession had a calming effect, especially after all those days in the remote wilderness.

Walking in the rain again, I went back to the transportation center. Especially odd to me was that the place had no seats, nothing at all. Bathrooms were on the outside, next to the police office. I also noticed the place would be locked each night at 10 p.m. If I couldn't get on the proper bus until 90 minutes after that, where was the best place to go? With some unusual characters inside the center and waiting for buses, I looked around. Two of them, a man and woman, had sleeping bags but were loud and a tad obnoxious. I headed back outside to walk back to the grocery store in search of a good book.

Inside the store, I found a very poor selection of books but a great answer from the cashier. With book in hand and a bag of peanuts, I asked the cashier how late the store was open. Midnight was the answer, so I had a comfortable area for waiting. Several small booths provided customers a place to eat what they had just purchased, and I was able to read and watch it rain.

As the time to head back for the late bus ride drew near, I noticed that the crowd kept coming into the store even as the evening cleanup processes began. When a worker started in the booth area, I began the walk back to the bus stop. The building was locked, along with the bathrooms, yet a dozen or so people were standing around outside or underneath the cover of a parking deck. Most were young and behaving. The sleeping bag couple were gone.

The time passed quickly and the bus I needed arrived precisely on time. I watched the driver shut off the bus and go inside the police office just as the other drivers did when they returned. When he came back out, he started the bus and opened the door. Everyone there moved to get on the last bus of the evening. I was glad to get this part of the journey going and remained excited about finally seeing the ferry.

I rode the bus as the rain poured, not sure when my stop would be. I just knew the driver had promised he would put me off at the farthest end of the route from where I would walk to the ferry. We made lots of stops, most in especially dark places. The Alaska sky was pitch dark with rain clouds, and I wondered what my stop would be like. We kept going, and I expected to be called forward at any time. I noticed the rain slowing and soon, so did the bus. At that stop, the driver looked at me and said, "This is your stop." I walked to the front, and asked, "Where from here?" He pointed down the road to the left. I already knew that the walk was about a mile and a half. I had plenty of time and looked forward to the walk. We had just passed midnight.

I began walking and saw almost no traffic, no stores open, and only a few houses. After about 10 minutes, I had seen no signs and watched as a taxi and another car pulled into an automated gasoline service that had no store, just the credit card pumps. I asked one of the drivers for directions to make sure I was on the right road. Right away, both drivers offered to take me the rest of the way. The taxi driver dropped me off at the brightly lit ferry terminal. "You can go on inside. They are open for business," he said. I thanked him and he drove on back to his work.

The ferry experience began with checking in. I was the fourth person who did so and had plenty of time to talk with the guy at the desk. He told me that the Columbia would begin boarding at 2:30 or 2:45 a.m. We talked about my bike ride and what it would be like onboard the ferry. Water travel has always been interesting to me. I love big ships. Just a couple hours later, I would be on one. Too excited to doze off, I was surprised that the others in the bright and increasingly busy room could sleep. Cars, vans and taxis began to arrive as they dropped off other passengers.

The check-in person told me that they would make an announcement when the ferry was ready to board. Nothing was ever said but people began to leave the room and not return. I gathered my things and walked on down to the boarding area. The ferry was in fact boarding and after showing my boarding pass and driver's license, I did the same. I walked through the huge cavern of the car, truck, bus and RV loading area, and followed the crew's directions up the stairs and into the ship. The crew was balancing the weight of the ship, apparently, as they had certain vehicles park specifically as they loaded.

My plan, what little there was of it, was to do the adventure thing that I had read about. I wanted to sleep outside on one of the upper decks. Outside in this case meant under a roof, but in the open air. Warm heat lamps were attached to the underside of that roof and they greatly warmed the area. I noticed right away that placement mattered and being positioned under two lamps was best. For sleeping, we had the long, hard pool-type plastic lounging chairs that lay out flat available. When I found the area, a handful of other passengers, probably those who were already on board, looked sound asleep.

I had brought my sleeping bag just for this purpose and made a bed on my chair. I used my pannier bag for a pillow and was soon squared away and fairly comfortable. I fell asleep in the quiet and peaceful environment quickly but soon awoke to see two women making up a more elaborate bed for themselves on two chairs beside me. They were silhouetted in the dark as they took way more care than I did. I was glad that no mosquitos gathered around. I had not explored the ship at all on the way up, knowing there would be plenty of time for that later. One spot on the chair was uncomfortable and I planned to fix that before the next night. I slept until 5 a.m. and never knew when the ferry left Juneau.

Other ports were ahead, including some where we could get off and visit the area. My ferry experience was limited, but I had been on others in the North Carolina system along the Outer Banks. This boat was by far the biggest ferry I had ever seen. The Columbia has a capacity of about 133 vehicles and 500 people and was built in 1976. I would be on it until early Friday morning, the day I planned to fly home.

The ferry had an upscale restaurant and a modest café, a theatre and an ocean-viewing lounge. Most of the passengers paid extra for a stateroom. Mine was the basic plan, which just covered the ride to Bellingham at $442. That included my passage on the boat and free showers. Meals were not included but were very affordable. To those who didn't pay to have a stateroom, sleeping was available in virtually any public place on the ship. Some people obviously traveled using the ferry often and were well versed in what they needed for a comfortable sleep.

I had breakfast in the restaurant the second morning and enjoyed the best view on the ship while eating. Still, my favorite place was the café, which was open 22 hours a day. I became a fan of their large scones for the first time ever. I bought three when leaving the ship.

Between stops to load and unload vehicles and people, we plied the same inland passage the big cruise ships do. Because of the intermittent and sometimes heavy rain, we never saw the tops of the mountains and glaciers along that portion. The water views were wonderful. We looked for whales and eagles mostly. An officer came by the viewing lounge every so often with information about what was ahead, time changes and any ship's news.

I mentioned the two women who set up their beds close to me. They got on in Juneau, same as me, and planned to drive to Texas and continue life there. The one nearer me in the sleeping arrangement was Maddy. The other lady owned the truck they were riding in, and Maddy had the contacts in Texas. I didn't know what they did before leaving Alaska, but Maddy was excited to head for a fresh beginning. Some type of disagreement occurred about the time they got on the ship and they stopped talking, with Maddy expecting to be booted from the truck, and the other woman no longer headed to Texas. Maddy kept sharing her thoughts about all this. I knew way more than I wanted to.

My time on the ferry was wonderful and restful. I had no big duties, no mountains to climb and no animals to avoid. I napped and ate, and I enjoyed the time in Sitka when we could get off the ferry and walk around. A bus took us to the edge of town. The area had interesting history and plenty of little shops that were not so touristy. I had Alaska fry bread, a native treat that can be savory or sweet, and loved it. Mine had just butter and plenty of calories.

Ketchikan was a poorly planned excursion. We were allowed to get off the ferry and supposed to have almost two hours of free time. With some sort of mechanical delay, we couldn't get off the ship until there was less than an hour and a half left. A couple dozen passengers took off walking toward downtown and never got past the industrial area before we had to turn around and return. I stopped in a Safeway grocery and grabbed a couple of Long Johns, another bicycle trip exclusive pastry. Then I had to walk back fast, making the cutoff by just three minutes. We never saw the pretty part of Ketchikan.

As the ferry trip was winding down, I spent more time watching the ocean from the front in the viewing lounge. I listened to conversations and occasionally talked to the people I met. One woman had actually been briefly on her bike within a day or two of where I was and would get back on her bike once we docked in Bellingham.

Intrigued a little by Maddy, I asked her how much money she had. She had less than $50. I bought her breakfast and gave her a little more. She got a ride to the bus station nearby. I haven't heard what happened. I never knew her last name.

On Friday morning, I was up and packed early. It didn't take long with my one bag. I got a shower at 5 a.m. and breakfast in the café. I was set for the shuttle to the airport and flights home to end my more than 50 days away. My shuttle from Bellingham was almost 45 minutes late, but I still made it to the Seattle airport 10 minutes early. That was the last on-time thing that happened while associated with the flights.

I checked in at the Seattle airport's Delta kiosk and learned my flight was delayed, with an undetermined new time. I picked another flight on the kiosk screen but realized the flight was scheduled for departure almost four hours before I got there. Thinking there was a mistake, I took the boarding pass straight to the trouble desk. I was second in line behind about 50 Korean teenagers. An agent helped the guy in front of me as the line backed up. Once he was cleared, I went straight to that agent. Yet another adventure was well underway!

The agent looked at my new boarding pass and called the gate, where he was told that the flight had been delayed all morning and was boarding then. Of course, it was in another terminal and I had yet to go through security. I asked the agent if I had a chance. He said, "Hurry, go to this security!" I ran that way and was immediately turned around by a TSA person who said this security point was closed. She directed us to the next one another terminal away.

Thinking I had no chance, I ran that way. The area was nearly as full, but multiple agents were hustling people through faster than I had ever seen passengers processed. Usually the TSA hassles me about a shoulder they say has metal in it. None of that this time. I grabbed my shoes and took off running again. I made it to the gate and asked if I was in fact on this flight now. This agent said, "You are!" Boarding continued as I took time to get a bottle of water and go to the bathroom. Just in time, I walked in with my group to my seat on the plane.

The people on this flight had been waiting to fly since early that morning, with a mechanical issue delaying take-off. They had been given Big Macs by the boxes and cases of water. I was still about an hour ahead of my original flight and felt like I was in good shape. Then we sat. After about 30 minutes, the pilot came on and said the plane had plenty of fuel but would need to be "balanced," something that would take 45 minutes. It took an hour. Now running later than the original intended flight, I knew I would miss my connection in Minneapolis. I sat and stewed, unsure of what to expect. I was fully aware that I may have to spend the night in the airport.

We arrived in Minneapolis to find that my 3:45 p.m. connection had been delayed and I could still get on it. That 3:45 p.m. turned into almost midnight, and we finally arrived in Charlotte at 4 a.m.

In a cruel twist of fate, the airline or airport had forgotten to arrange a gate for us to deplane. Another 15-minute delay got us off the plane about 4:20. An Uber ride dropped me at home at 5:20 a.m. The first thing I did was go for a short run, my first in 46 days. It was miserable! But I was not. I had made it home, completed all my goals and felt wonderful!

Leaving Mission Senior Living in Carson City, Nevada.

The closed rest area in California with a free flowing spring when Freeze needed water.

208

Firefighter Ryan Rodd gave Freeze food and water in California. Rodd is from Greensboro, N.C.

The Harris Schoolhouse near Summer Lake, Oregon was first opened in 1890.

Canadian
Customs
Officer
Williams
helped
Freeze
change to a
safer route.

Freeze enters British Columbia.

Bear-proof trash receptacles in British Columbia.

The last stagecoach from the British Columbia Express. It is displayed at 100 Mile House.

The populace of Cinema, B.C. One house and one small store.

Freeze dressed for a cold day on the bike and B.C. 97.

With Wayne Eller, formerly of Rowan County, in Burns Lake, B.C.

Four French cyclists riding from Anchorage to Argentina on a yearlong journey.

The Bulkley-Nechako Glacier near Smithers, B.C.

The old baseball field in Moricetown, B.C.

Spectacular mountains near New Hazelton, B.C.

The Bell Irving River.

Sunrise on Dease Lake on the Cassiar Highway.

Julien and Frederick Gailliard from Belgium told Freeze he most likely wouldn't make Anchorage by July 12. He did.

216

Entering the Yukon and joining the Alaska Highway.

The bear! Freeze wanted to see a grizzly and the first one in the Yukon chased him.

217

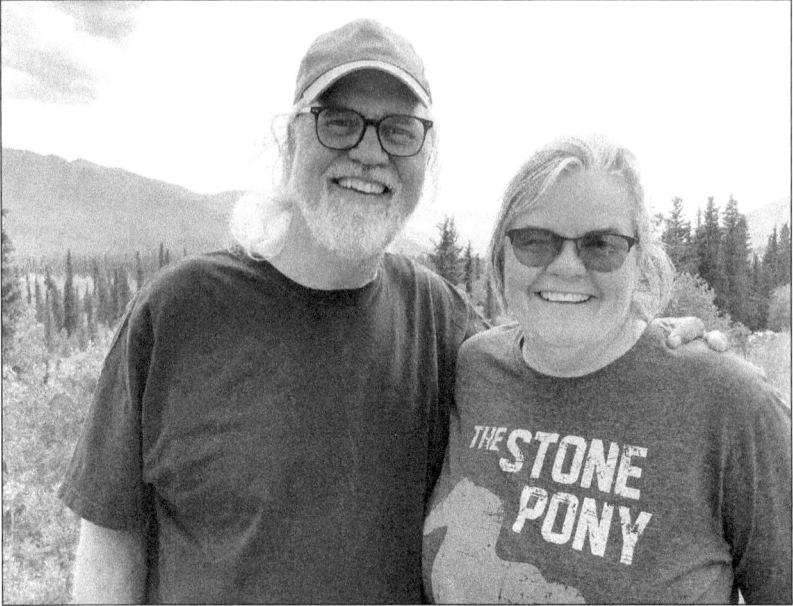

Lee and Jeannie Kanter gave Freeze water from their RV on another warm day away from supply points.

The SS Klondike, a historic ore carrier, on display in downtown Whitehorse, the Yukon.

218

Freeze asked directions of Deb Jutra in Whitehorse and then she found him two more times later that same day with directions and information.

These women were hiking near Haines Junction and stopped Freeze. He got snacks and an offer for lunch.

Abel from Cadence Cycle checked out a bike issue for Freeze right away and only charged for parts.

Mountains and Alaska Highway near Haines Junction, B.C.

220

Bryan Troll, of Philadelphia, provided water from his RV on one of Freeze's hardest travel days.

Entering Alaska and capturing Freeze's 49th state on a bicycle.

Pete from the Nelchina Lodge saved Freeze a room even though he was four hours late.

Freeze spent the night in a 100-year-old settler's cabin at Red Eagle Lodge.

Juan Jerez of San Jose, California passed Freeze multiple times on the trip. He was going to Argentina after Alaska and planned to travel for a year.

Note the height of the mail-box.

Roman Durren of Oberegg, Switzerland, spent the previous night under a bridge.

The patrol car in Teslin, the Yukon.

Frank and Janis Ramsey at their home near Wasilla, Alaska, where Freeze spent his last night on the road. Frank Ramsey is from Salisbury, N.C.

Freeze was glad that Anchorage recognized his nearly 3,200-mile journey.

Freeze traveled from Juneau, Alaska, back to Bellingham, Washington, on the Columbia, flagship of the Alaska ferry system.

Amber and her husband Jamie in Anchorage.

EPILOGUE

Looking back isn't as easy for me as looking forward. I'm already thinking about what's next. But now that I am in a quiet place, with most of this book complete, it's just fine to reminisce about nearly 3,200 miles from Carson City, Nevada, to Anchorage, Alaska.

People often ask, "Do you ever just think of quitting? Giving it up and going home?" Not one single time has that thought ever crossed my mind. But I will admit that this ride took all the perseverance I could muster at times. Never before has the average riding day been so long and the mileage per day been this high. This adventure had the highest highs, the lowest lows and the most challenges ever. But with my thirst for adventure, I wouldn't have wanted to miss a minute of it.

Back at the Petro Canada store at the start of the Cassiar Highway, Buffalo Bill's lookalike probably said it best: "You must be a stupid son of a bitch to think that you can ride that road on a bicycle. It ain't safe, I tell you!" He said a lot more too, and he may have been right. However, the biggest decision I had to make during the first half of the ride was whether to take the safer Alaska Highway or the wildest road in western Canada. Several people tried to convince me to take the safer route. Just like every other adventure, I wanted it all. If I never visit the area again, I'm all right with that. Simply because I did the Cassiar Highway.

From Nevada to Anchorage, the scenery was just as expected: often spectacular and occasionally mundane. The roads were the worst I have ridden as a whole. But the weather was better than usual, with only two crazy big thunderstorms over the 39 days. Just 10 minutes of hail reminded me of what could have been. Winds were probably the worst yet overall, simply because they changed so often. I have seen short duration headwinds in Kansas that were much worse. From a low of 28 degrees to a high of 96, nothing about the weather overwhelmed me. The most memorable event was crossing through an active forest fire in eerie silence, just me alone. Some would say the bear chase should take that prize, but I never worried about that situation. Maybe it happened too fast and my prayers comforted me. Still, I am glad he didn't catch up.

I didn't have the informative maps from some of the previous trips, but I had way fewer roads and a great publication called Milepost. And I had helpful people along the way, time and again — from Officer Williams at Canadian Customs and the Andrews couple at the Camaray Motel, to

Frank and Janis Ramsey near Wasilla, Alaska. Valuable help came forward time and again. Joe Troyer, Deb Jutra and Pete at Nelchina provide great memories of the goodness of people who live far away, but are brought much closer by their common goodness.

Some of that help, as usual, came from home. Getting connectivity eventually kept the newspaper updates going. It also helped me stay in touch with friends, old and new, who offered suggestions and support. The biggest connection for me, said time and again, is to the people, those that I already know and those I meet for the first time as a sidebar to every adventure.

Sleeping in the bed of a truck on the first night and upgrading to a pile of gravel the next should have warned me of crazy things to come. Long daylight made for many miles on certain days. Twice I was still riding near midnight, which happened to be about the only time I could be sure of outdistancing the mosquitos and flies.

The stifling dust of constant repaving was something I didn't expect. Neither did I foresee the extremely high prices in many areas. I didn't think my tent would fall apart, either, especially while camping in areas with bear scat nearby.

On the fun side, I learned about butter tarts, Long Johns and Mr. Big candy bars. Ice isn't usually available in this part of the world. And it's hard to see the Northern Lights when it doesn't get dark. Never having seen a bear or a rattlesnake in the open before, I quickly realized that my eyes had to be open and my mind focused — again, probably more so than ever before.

I practiced speed camping set up and break down due to the mosquito alert system, never bought bear spray and still felt safe all the way.

So, what is coming next? First thing, none of the post-ride blood clots have yet been an issue, so I hope they stay away. As far as I can tell, my feet and everything else have healed, save for a sort of tennis elbow that still lingers a few months after the ride.

The bike arrived home with a few pieces missing but is ready again. I am too, with a small plan and a bigger one starting to take shape. I have crossed America through its middle and its northern tier, and for some reason the southern tier is on my mind. Possibly San Francisco to St. Augustine, Florida, just north of the Mexican border and the Gulf of Mexico, all states I have seen but roads not yet ridden.

And the 50th state is out there, still to be conquered. The plan as I write this is to visit Hawaii and ride, probably in March of 2020.

No doubt, I am one fortunate and sometimes lucky guy, with lots of blessings to count. The wanderlust is building already and it won't be long until some adventure has to start. I can't wait to hit the road! And as always, I hope each of you will join me, yet again!

GEAR LIST

Many of the items that I carried on the bike trip to Alaska had made multiple trips before. Over the years, I have weighed several factors when considering what to take. Each item must serve a purpose, have a reasonable weight and take up as little space as possible. When I first considered the cross-country trip in 2013, I spoke with Andrew Sufficool at length about his preferences. Andrew had made several trips by that time, some with his brother, Matt. I now carry less than they did when touring.

I valued Andrew's experience, and he was willing to share his knowledge. I am doing the same for readers of the book, should anyone seriously be interested in a cycling trip of their own. On my trips, I often see cyclists with four major bags, two on the front axle and two on the back. I also occasionally see a large bag laid across the top of the rear panniers. Most cyclists also have a handlebar bag, usually for those items that are needed quickly on occasion. I have also seen "under the bar" frame bags and "under the saddle" bags. My point in sharing this is that there are many ways to mount bags on a bike and lots of items on the market that may benefit cyclists.

First-time endurance touring cyclists often carry too much, both in weight and space needed. Having camped at a higher percentage on this trip than any previous one, I tested out my own theories of what needed to go and what needed to stay home. The last month before leaving was spent assessing and reassessing my gear. What follows are the major items that made the trip, by manufacturer, how many trips made and whether the item performed satisfactorily.

Foremost was the Surly Long Haul Trucker bicycle. This is the second model I have owned after the first was totaled in a wreck in Florida near the end of the trip from Maine to Key West. The Surly LHT is made for the rigors of distance touring. It is a tough, smooth-riding bike that can carry way more weight than I need. I read the other day that it can carry a 300-pound rider and 55 pounds of weight. I weigh about 140 and often carry 40-50 pounds in just two bags on the back axle, and a medium-sized handlebar bag. The same B-17 Brooks saddle has been on both bikes. Although I don't take especially take good care of it, the leather seat is very comfortable to me. The bike is the old style with regular brakes and currently has 27 gears. I used caged pedals on all my rides.

One important accessory for the bike is the Sigma bike computer. I use the basic one, currently the BC5.16, not really interested in the super data that I don't have time to compute. I just want actual speed, trip distance, total distance and ride time. The 24-hour clock is nice too.

Another accessory is the Planet Bike rear rack. Always sturdy, this same style rack has made all my trips but was replaced new after the Florida wreck.

The final pieces on the bike are Planet Bike fenders. These fenders keep the underneath of the rider drier and less messy in wet conditions. I wouldn't go riding without them.

All my bags are made by Ortlieb. The panniers are the originals from my first ride, although both are scratched and scraped from the Florida wreck and plenty of use. The handlebar bag was brand new for this trip and has a magnetic closure for the first time. The old bag had elastic snaps that eventually broke and took longer to open. All the bags are waterproof. I don't like the fact that the new handlebar bag does not have inside pockets, as the old one did.

I use a map case from Adventure Cycling that mounts to the handlebars and sits above and to the rear of the handlebar bag. Some handlebar bags have the map case made into the top cover.

My sleeping bag is the 40-degree one made by Field and Stream, and it has been on all the trips except the first cross-country trip. It packs tight and can ride in one of the panniers or on top of them. Early on this trip, I thought I made a mistake by not bringing the heavier bag, but I quickly settled things by wearing more clothes to bed.

The air mattress is a roll-up style that you inflate by blowing into it. It is only about four feet long. The manufacturer is Thermarest, and it's the Scout style. The mattress is hard to blow up but inflates enough to be marginally comfortably on all but the roughest ground.

The last item on my "returning" list were my Nike leather gloves. Nearly totally worn out, they will be the symbol of longevity during my Hawaiian ride in 2020. The gloves have survived a lot. They are worn through in spots but still protect the hands from the all-day abrasion of the handlebars. The mid-finger on down is open.

My new iPad Mini Version 5 was a big hit. Photo quality and ability to get texts on it were pluses. I find the iPad Mini easy to type on and hope to get five years out of this one, just as I did with the Version 2.

Also new this year was a Sawyer Squeeze kit for filtering water from streams. I didn't have to use it but feel confident it would be safe. Just gather water in the plastic containers provided and lightly squeeze it through the filter to drink or catch in a container on the other side.

Another new item, my improved rain jacket, was a purchase from Amazon from a manufacturer called Arro Where. The jacket is bright yellow, with a big reflective safety emblem on the back. I bought a small and it fit like a glove and served as an extra layer of warmth on cold evenings. The big plus was a nice pocket to put things in, while the only negative was no hood. The collar was nice but a hood extension would have been even better. The yellow jacket was black with grime in places by the time I could wash it at home.

New too were my bike shorts. For the first time, I wore a pair with loose fitting legs and pockets, both big winners. Another purchase from Amazon, the shorts have no name that's still readable. Zippered side pockets and one Velcro pocket for a bigger item on one leg were big pluses. I wore this same pair every day for 39 long days of riding and they show no wear.

Two more new purchases were the Even Naturals mosquito net from Amazon and the Sport floppy hat from 7-Eleven. Both did a wonderful job, but I didn't use the net as much as I should have. Setting up and taking down the tent was the best time for its use, but even then a few mosquitos got inside. I was told later to tuck the bottom part in my jacket to solve this problem. A good lesson learned.

The best feature of the floppy hat was a draw band along the circumference of hat, instead of one hanging down the neck. The hat was easy to adjust, stayed on in heavy wind, was comfortable to wear and shielded my face and most of my neck from the sun and rain.

I carried two cell phone-size solar chargers on this trip, one new and one used. Neither did a good job of charging in the sun but each one stored enough juice to charge my iPhone and iPad both one time. I never ran short of battery power. Usually I just charged them where I had power instead of waiting on the very slow solar charge.

On to the tools, pump and accessories. I carried a small tool kit, the same as always. It consists of a complete set of allen wrenches, the CO_2 inflator and the plastic tire levers used to take off and put on tires when changing a tube. I change tubes and never patch one. Patched tubes often are going to need to be patched again, and the trial and delay required to get back on the road should be limited as much as possible.

Three new items for the tool kit this time included Finish Line 1-Step cleaner and lubricant. Bike shops didn't happen often on this trip, so I carried my own lubricant. I also bought a used chain connector tool and a quick repair link just in case the chain broke in the wilderness.

I do carry a small bike pump but haven't used it in the last three trips. It barely has the capacity for inflating the tire to minimum levels for supporting the weight of the bike, gear and me. But it will work in an emergency. On the next trip, this pump may not make the cut, as the CO_2 inflation is much easier, faster and more dependable.

The last big item that I want to mention is the tent. I have used two tents on my trips over the years. The first one leaked out of the box, within a week after purchase, and never was the right choice anyway. The second one made six years without leaking, but it has now come apart in some key places. Before my next long trip, I will be considering another tent. Make sure you look for quality, read reviews, ask questions and consider weight and space taken. Tents are good to ride on top the frame carrier, between the clipped-on panniers. Get a demonstration on how long it takes to put up the tent and take it back down.

Clothing and hygiene products make up the rest of my list. I usually take a pair of flip-flops for showers, a small towel, the usual toiletries and a selection of clothing. A long sleeve T-shirt, a couple of short sleeve ones in bright colors and a couple pairs of socks are the basics. My only addition is a wool, long sleeve shirt that can aid in warmth as needed. On most trips, I carry a pair of long running pants with zippered ankles. These are good for sleeping or cold riding. Mittens are great for the real cold that I experienced on this ride.

That leaves the helmet, something I change just about every long-distance trip. I still am not completely happy with what I have and will be on the lookout for the one that really fits.

With all of these items, personal preference and expense matter. I met one cyclist from Japan as he was headed to Argentina. He had the best and newest of everything, and was on his first long-distance ride. One of the first things we talked about was his overweight load. "I have way too much stuff," he said. I agreed!

After 49 states, I still don't know what would fill four bags on my bike. I cannot think of one single additional item I needed on this Alaska trip. But each singular cyclist has his preferences. It was once explained to me, "Take along a bunch of stuff and you have to pedal it up the hills. You'll figure out real quick what you need!" That's sage advice.

ABOUT THE AUTHOR

Just two states remained. Sure that Alaska and the long route from Nevada to Anchorage would provide major challenges, especially those remote areas of British Columbia and the Yukon, David Freeze set out to capture state number 49. This is the author's eighth book.

David is also a motivational speaker, emphasizing that regular people can achieve amazing things. Contact him at david.freeze@ctc.net. Walnut Creek Farm Publishing is named after his farm.

An accomplished runner and endurance cyclist, David has written five other books that cover various adventures across America by bicycle and one by historic biplane. He has completed nearly 86,000 running miles and over 20,000 endurance cycling miles.

Other books by David Freeze include:

- **Lord, Ride with Me Today**
  The story of a solo coast-to-coast bicycle journey — 2013

- **Pedaling, Prayers and Perseverance**
  35 Days Cycling Solo from Maine to Key West — 2014

- **Riding the Rails to Freedom**
  Cycling the Underground Railroad Route from Alabama to Ontario — 2015

- **Highway to History**
  A Cycling Adventure on Route 66 — 2016

- **Young Again**
  Veterans recapture a moment of youth through Ageless Aviation Dreams Foundation — 2017

- **Cycling the Northwest**
  A solo trip from the West Coast to Green Bay, through Bigfoot country — 2017

- **One Day at a Time Across North Carolina**
  A solo run/walk behind a baby jogger — 2018

www.ingramcontent.com/pod-product-compliance
Lightning Source LLC
LaVergne TN
LVHW051624080426
835511LV00016B/2156